D1337981

THE IRELAND RUGBY MISCELLANY

THE IRELAND RUGBY MISCELLANY

BY CIARAN CRONIN

Vision Sports Publishing
2 Coombe Gardens,
London, SW20 0QU

www.visionsp.co.uk

Published by Vision Sports Publishing. 2007

Text © Ciaran Cronin
Illustrations © Bob Bond Sporting Caricatures

ISBN 10: 1-905326-25-4
ISBN 13: 978-1-905326-25-9

All rights reserved. No part of this publication may be reproduced, stored in a retrieval system, or transmitted in any form or by any means, electronic, mechanical, photocopying, recording or otherwise, without the prior permission of the publishers.

This book is sold subject to the condition that it shall not, by way of trade or otherwise, be lent, re-sold, hired out, or otherwise circulated without the publisher's prior consent in any form of binding or cover other than that in which it is published and without a similar condition including this condition being imposed on the subsequent purchaser.

Printed and bound in the UK by
Cromwell Press Ltd, Trowbridge, Wiltshire

Typeset by Palimpsest Book Production Limited,
Grangemouth, Stirlingshire

A CIP catalogue record for this book is
available from the British Library

Vision Sports Publishing are proud that this book is made from paper certified by the Forest Stewardship Council

Foreword
By Willie John McBride

It's a great privilege to write the foreword to a book that is not only full of facts, figures and trivia of Irish rugby's past, but also acts as a short history of the game in this country. Over the past decade Irish rugby has gained countless new fans from all corners of the country and this book will help anybody new to the game to gain a real understanding to the players, teams and stories that have passed before.

I earned my first Irish cap back in 1962 against England at Twickenham and from then, until my retirement in 1975, I experienced some incredible moments in both the Irish and Lions jerseys.

This book does have the odd reference or two to myself, but facts and figures were never something I was all that bothered about during my playing career. Most of us were simply happy to be playing rugby and representing our country, while getting to see a bit of the world at the same time. In saying that, some moments do stand out.

I was very aware that my try against France in my final game at Lansdowne Road was my very first in an Irish jersey and I suppose it's ironic that it came on such a special day for me. People forget, however, that I scored plenty of tries throughout my career, even if they weren't in the green of Ireland.

The *This is Your Life* moment, mentioned later on in these pages, is also something I'll never forget. I got such a shock when Eamonn Andrews came over to me after the Centenary fixture at Lansdowne Road and the evening spent recording the programme in the Shelbourne Hotel was a wonderful experience.

There are other stories here that will no doubt catch your eye. I find it hard to believe that Dolman Walkington, an Irish full-back in the late 19th century, wore a monocle when playing and that he used to remove his viewing piece when taking a kick at goal. One thing I know for sure is that he wouldn't have lasted all that long out in South Africa on a Lions, or any other sort of tour. Then there's the story of John Macauley, a Limerick man, who decided to get married just so he could get a day off work to play for Ireland. There's dedication and then there's dedication on a different level entirely!

It's also interesting to see that all the old names in the records books are fast disappearing. Malcolm O'Kelly is Ireland's most-capped player, while Ronan O'Gara has scored the most points for his country. The fact of the matter is that nobody from my era can really compete with these guys because of the amount of internationals that are played nowadays. I played an average of five internationals per year during my time in an Irish jersey. Today's top players play at least double that.

Anyway, I hope you enjoy dipping in and out of Ciaran Cronin's book and I'm sure there will be enough interesting, humorous and downright bizarre stories to keep you amused for a while to come.

Willie John McBride

Acknowledgements

There are a number of people who deserve thanks for their help with this book.

To Paul Morgan of *Rugby World* magazine for first getting me involved with this project, and to Jim Drewett and Toby Trotman of Vision Sports Publishing for their professionalism and good humour over the past couple of months.

Also, thanks to Andie for her love and patience during a second summer in-a-row of writing and to my parents Mary and Mike, for all their help down the years.

As with all books of this type, the odd omission and inaccuracy will occur. Please try not to let it drive you mad and I would be extremely appreciative if you could contact me through the publishers if you either happen to discover an error or omission, or if you know of any story that might be of interest for future editions of the book.

Enjoy the read,

Ciaran Cronin

Author's Notes: Please note that all point tallies in this book were compiled on the basis of five points for try, three for a penalty and drop-goal and two for a conversion. If a player competed in an era where a different points system applied, his points have been converted to comply with modern-day scoring.

All facts and figures in this book are correct as of 3 September 2007.

— AN IRISHMAN INVENTS THE GAME? —

The tale of how rugby was invented, and who was responsible for that "fine disregard" for the rules of football, is well known but what has been brushed under the carpet is the doubt surrounding the nationality of William Webb Ellis himself. Most organs of the British Empire would have us believe that Webb Ellis was born in Manchester in 1806, but that supposed fact has never been fully verified. Without any official documents around to prove his English birth, the possibility remains that Webb Ellis was actually born in Ireland.

In the year of his birth, Webb Elllis' father, James, was an officer in the Dragoon Regiment of the British Army and records show that the family spent time in Dundalk, Dublin and Clonmel, County Tipperary in the year of William's birth. It is also known that William had numerous cousins in Clonmel and even if it can't be confirmed he was born there himself, he did spend many summers in Ireland visiting his relations. It has been suggested by historians that William would have played caid – a primitive form of Gaelic football – during his time in Ireland and that he was merely demonstrating to his school chums this strange and unusual game when he reputedly invented rugby back in 1823.

— WHEN TWO BECAME ONE —

On 12 December 1874 the Irish Football Union (IFU) was formed in Dublin, closely followed by the formation of the Northern Football Union (NFU) in Belfast in January 1875. Both unions shared the responsibility for selecting the first series of Irish teams to play international rugby, but it wasn't until 1879 that the two unions finally agreed to merge. The new organisation, entitled the Irish Rugby Football Union (IRFU), held its first meeting on 5 February 1880 at 63 Grafton Street in Dublin, with Dr William Neville elected as the union's first ever president.

Since then, and despite the partition of the country in subsequent years, quite remarkably neither politics nor religion has unduly interfered in the running of the IRFU.

— IRELAND'S FIRST CLUBS —

Trinity College are not only Ireland's oldest club, they are also reputed to be the second oldest club in the world behind Guy's Hospital of London. The first records of rugby at the university come from 1854, when a group of former English public schoolboys decided to introduce the locals to the game of their respective youths.

For years Trinity struggled for opposition and were forced to play in-house games between themselves until the former public school boys, and thus the game, spread across the rest of the country. Below is a list of the clubs that came after Trinity:

Club	Formed
Wanderers	1860
North of Ireland FC	1868
Queen's University	1869
Wanderers RFC	1870*
Lansdowne	1872
Dungannon	1873
Carlow	1873
Queens College Cork	1874
Ballinasloe	1875
Limerick County	1876

**Present day Wanderers club*

— POINTS VALUE —

A number of different points systems have been used in Irish rugby through the years, with the last change taking place in the summer of 1992.

	Try	Conversion	Penalty	Drop
1871 to 1891	1	2	2	3
1892 to 1893	2	3	3	4
1894 to 1895	3	2	3	4
1896 to 1971	3	2	3	3
1972 to 1991	4	2	3	3
1992 to present	5	2	3	3

— THE SEX NATIONS —

Ireland's sexiest man

In March of 2004 Irish captain Brian O'Driscoll was named 'Ireland's Sexiest Man' by *Social & Personal* magazine, beating off competition from such screen legends as Colin Farrell and Pierce Brosnan. The only bone of contention surrounding his award was the fact that his then girlfriend, model Glenda Gilson, was one of the five judges who decided on the winner. Not that it bothered O'Driscoll one bit.

— FOLLOWING IN THEIR FATHERS' FOOTSTEPS —

The following father and sons have represented Ireland at international level:

Father	Years	Son(s)	Years
Frederick Schute	1878–79	Geoffrey Schute	1913
William Collis	1884	William Collis	1924–26
Coo Clinch	1885–97	Jamie Clinch	1924–31
George Collopy	1891–92	William Collopy	1914–24
		Dick Collopy	1923–25
Samuel Irwin	1900–03	John Irwin	1938–39
Tom Hewitt	1924–26	Dave Hewitt	1958–65
Paul Murray	1927–33	John Murray	1963
Morgan Crowe	1929–34	James Crowe	1974
Noel Murphy	1930–33	Noel Murphy	1958–69
Seamus Deering	1935–37	Shay Deering	1974–78
Harry McKibbin	1938–39	Christopher McKibbin	1976
		Alistair McKibbin	1977–80
Brendan Foley	1976–81	Anthony Foley	1995–2005
Des Fitzgerald	1984–92	Luke Fitzgerald	2006–

— IRELAND'S TRIPLE CROWNS: NO. 1, 1894 —

An away win over England is always a good way to get a campaign going and after Ireland defeated Scotland 5–0 at Lansdowne Road, the scene was set for the country's first ever Triple Crown, and by extension, Championship success. The crucial game was played against Wales at the Ballynafeigh Grounds in Belfast and a John Lytle penalty was enough to create Ireland's little bit of history, 19 years after their very first international fixture.

Date	Result	Venue
3 Feb 1894	England 5–7 Ireland	Blackheath
24 Feb 1894	Ireland 5–0 Scotland	Lansdowne Road
10 March 1894	Ireland 3–0 Wales	Ballynafeigh, Belfast

— FUJI CROAK IN SUVA —

Ireland have played just one match away to Fiji but it is unlikely to be one they'll forget.

On the way back from their 1975 tour to New Zealand, a tired Irish side arrived in Fiji's capital Suva only to discover that the island's international side weren't actually there. In an apparent scheduling mix-up, Fiji were in Australia playing a couple of friendly games but the IRFU's blushes were spared when the Fiji Rugby Union assembled a scratch side to play Ireland. Predictably enough, the tourists beat what was effectively a Fiji 'B' side 8–0 but most of Ireland's weary players remember the game for different reasons. Not only was the weather unbearably hot on the day of the game in the Fijian capital, but Ireland's internationals also had to contend with dozens of frogs hopping all over the pitch as they attempted to finish off their tour with a victory.

— NATIVES MAKE THEIR IRISH MARK —

They are now called the New Zealand Maoris, but back in 1888 they were called the New Zealand Natives and their arrival on Irish soil in November of that year signalled the beginning of the rugby touring tradition. The Natives were led by Joe Warbrick and although the Ireland players that faced them at Lansdowne Road on 1 December weren't awarded full caps for the occasion, a decent crowd turned up to catch a glimpse of the exotic visitors.

Unsurprisingly, the physically bigger visitors won the game 13–0, but the tourists did lose to both England and Wales over the course of their tour. Having left Auckland in June 1888, the touring Natives returned to New Zealand in August 1889, and the history books claim that they played 107 matches in Ireland, Britain and Australia over the course of their 14 months overseas. Bet that hurt.

— WILLIE OR WON'T HE? —

The All Blacks 'Haka' has been faced in a number of different ways by opposing teams down the years, but back in 1989 Willie Anderson's Irish side became the first side to almost come to blows with their opponents. As the All Blacks started their war dance at Lansdowne Road, the Irish team linked arms and slowly began advancing towards the Kiwis. In a matter of seconds, both teams were within a few inches of each other, with respective captains Wayne Shelford and Anderson little more than a hair's breadth apart. The Lansdowne Road crowd roared their approval at their team's response but thankfully both sides separated before they could come to blows.

"The All Blacks were getting all the cheers as they were doing the Haka," said Anderson of the incident. "So we decided that if we met them head-to-head, the crowd would get behind us. It worked too. The atmosphere at the game was fantastic. We were really inspired, and played way above ourselves." No matter how inspired they were with their pre-match defiance, it made no difference to the result, with the All Blacks winning 23–6.

— IRELAND LEGENDS: KEITH WOOD —

The inspirational Keith Wood

It is difficult to think of a more inspirational Irish rugby player than Keith Wood. The Clare native, a student of the famed St Munchin's College in Limerick, earned 58 caps over the course of his nine-year international career, but he would undoubtedly have been somewhere up towards the century mark had he not showed such reckless disregard for his own body on the field of play.

Wood threw himself into every ruck and every tackle as though his life depended on it, something that marked him out as a future Irish captain from an early age, even if it did land him on the physiotherapist's table for long periods. Allied to the physical side of his game, Wood possessed no little skill and he kicked the ball – be that garryowens, touchfinders or grubbers – more than any other hooker in world rugby. His penchant for the unknown annoyed a fair few traditionalists out there but watching Wood play the game was far from a boring experience.

His career started in Limerick, where Wood helped Garryowen to two All-Ireland League titles in 1992 and 1994, before crossing the water to join Harlequins in time for the 1994/95 season. He did come back to play for Munster in the 1999/00 season – a season in which his home province lost a Heineken Cup final to Northampton at Twickenham – but he returned to the Stoop the following year and played out the rest of his club career in south-west London.

But it is for his international escapades, both with Ireland and the Lions, that Wood is best remembered. While his work around the field was always more impressive than his line-out throwing, Wood was the starting test hooker on the Lions' series win over South Africa in 1997, a position he retained for the 2–1 series defeat in Australia four years later. Although he was in and out of the Irish team after his debut in 1994 – his erratic line-out throwing, in particular, an irritant for successive Irish coaches – Wood eventually established himself as starting hooker and captained his country for the first time against Australia in November 1996. He was handed the armband on a more permanent basis after Ireland's disastrous 1999 World Cup exit to Argentina in Lens, and his leadership played a key role in lifting Ireland from the depression of that defeat.

After battling with a shoulder injury throughout 2002 and the early part of 2003, Wood returned just in time for Ireland's 2003 World Cup campaign, where he led his country to the quarter-final stage. Following a heavy defeat to France at that point in the competition, Wood announced his retirement immediately after the game at the age of 31, with Brian O'Driscoll taking over as Irish captain.

On hanging up this boots, Wood had an impressive list of achievements to look back on from his rugby days. His 15 test tries established him as world rugby's highest scoring hooker, while he also won the inaugural IRB World Player of the Year award in 2001. Wood now works as an occasional rugby pundit for the BBC and lives with his wife and children in London.

Keith Gerard Mallinson Wood
Born: 27 January 1972, Killaloe, County Clare
Clubs: Garryowen and Harlequins
Caps: 58
Scoring: 75 points (15 tries)
Ireland debut: 15 January 1994 v Australia (Brisbane)

— FIRST OVER THE LINE —

John Loftus Cuppaidge of Trinity College was the first Irish man to score a try for his country. The medical student who went on to set up his own practice in Queensland, Australia, made his mark on Irish rugby history on 24 March 1880 against England at Lansdowne Road, a full five years after Ireland played their first international. The only pity about Loftus Cuppaidge's effort was that R.B. Wilkinson missed the conversion right in front of the posts, handing victory to England and leaving Ireland with a record of eight defeats from eight games.

— AND THEY ARE OFF, EARLY —

On 24 March 1913, the Ireland and France match in the Five Nations Championship at the Mardyke in Cork was played in the morning to allow spectators and both teams to attend the Cork races in the afternoon. The change of time didn't bother Ireland one bit, particularly J.P. Quinn, who scored a hat-trick of tries in a 24–0 win for the home side.

— HOMES AT HOME —

Ireland have played home games at ten different venues around the country. Below is a list of the results in full test games at those grounds:

Venue	First game	W	L	D
Ballynafeigh (Belfast)	21 Feb 1891 v Scotland	4	7	0
Balmoral (Belfast)	19 Feb 1898 v Scotland	4	6	0
Croke Park	11 Feb 2007 v France	1	1	0
Ennis Road (Limerick)	19 March 1898 v Wales	0	1	0
Lansdowne Road	11 March 1878 v England	102	108	17
Mardyke (Cork)	25 March 1911 v France	3	0	0
Ormeau Road (Belfast)	19 Feb 1887 v Scotland	1	5	0
Rathmines (Dublin)	13 Dec 1875 v England	0	1	0
Ravenhill	9 Feb 1924 v England	10	5	1
Thomond Park	7 Sept 2002 v Romania	2	0	0

— CAP IN TIME —

New South Wales provided Ireland's first taste of Australian opposition back in 1927. The touring side beat a full Irish side and in recognition of their achievement, the Australian Rugby Union retrospectively awarded Test status to the match and international caps to the players in 1987, fully 60 years later.

— GOD SAVE THE ROSE OF TRALEE —

Anthems have sometimes been a controversial issue in Irish rugby, but what occurred during Ireland's World Cup campaign of 1987 was purely comical.

An IRB decree before the start of the tournament stating that all teams must play a national anthem before games caught the IRFU cold and an official was hastily dispatched to the music stores of Wellington to find a tape with some kind of Irish song on it. All he could find was a tape which included 'The Rose of Tralee' – a traditional Irish love song – and it was duly played before Ireland's World Cup games in New Zealand and Australia.

The ballad's mournful lament didn't exactly fire the players up before heading into battle but it did lead to some interesting notions on future anthems, including the suggestion from journalist Con Houlihan that 'God Save the Rose of Tralee' could be used before future Irish games.

The Rose Of Tralee

The pale moon was rising above the green mountain
The sun was declining beneath the blue sea
When I strayed with my love to the pure crystal fountain
That stands in beautiful vale of Tralee.
She was lovely and fair as the rose of the summer
Yet, 'twas not her beauty alone that won me
Oh no! 'Twas the the truth in her eye ever beaming
That made me love Mary, the Rose of Tralee.

— IN BUSINESS —

Monday 15 February 1875 was the date, the Kennington Oval in London the venue. Ireland travelled to face England in their first international fixture but there were some complications.

With two Unions in the country, the IFU and the NFU, the team was selected on a representative basis. There were 20 players on a team back then, seven from the north, seven from the south and six others chosen by a team of selectors from both unions. The Dublin based IFU, by hook or by crook, eventually ended up with 12 players on the pitch, nine of them from Trinity College, but the home side won the game by two goals and try to nil.

Ireland were a good deal off the pace in their first international but at least they were in business.

— IRELAND'S FIRST BOYCOTT —

The late 19th century was a messy period for international rugby. In 1888 and 1889, England were barred from entering the home championship because of their refusal to accept the newly formed International Board, while in August 1895 the Northern Rugby League was formed after an argument in England over whether rugby players should be paid.

Then came the Arthur Gould affair. Gould was Wales' star man of the era and in 1897, as he was coming towards the end of his career, the centre was presented with a house in recognition of his contribution to Welsh rugby. Even though the Welsh Rugby Union had not directly organised the fund to purchase Gould's house, both Ireland and Scotland saw the handover of the property as an act of professionalism and refused to play Wales that year. The dispute was only solved when the player retired.

— THE TEN TRIES OR MORE CLUB —

The full list of players who have scored ten or more tries for Ireland:

Player		Career	Tries
1=	Denis Hickie	1997–	29
1=	Brian O'Driscoll	1999–	29
3	Shane Horgan	2000–	20
4=	Girvan Dempsey	1998–	17
4=	Brendan Mullin	1984–1995	17
4=	Geordan Murphy	2000–	17
7=	Kevin Maggs	1997–2005	15
7=	Keith Wood	1994–2003	15
9	George Stephenson	1920–1930	14
10	Ronan O'Gara	2000–	13
11	Keith Crossan	1982–1992	12
12=	Alan Duggan	1963–1973	11
12=	Simon Geoghegan	1991–1996	11
14	Hugo McNeill	1981–1988	10

— THE IRISH PACK COMES OF AGE —

It is difficult to believe it now but in the early part of the 20th century, the Irish pack were seen as a bunch of softies, an eight who were rarely up for the fight and often ran out of what little steam they possessed well before the final whistle.

That attitude, however, began to change following Ireland's 6–6 draw against England at Twickenham in 1925. Before that particular encounter, England had won every game they'd played against Ireland since as far back as 1911 but on the afternoon in question, a George Beamish-inspired Irish pack fought for their lives and kept going right until the end.

"The game was marked by the happy and strange phenomenon," it was noted in one report by *The Times* of London afterwards, "of an Irish pack of forwards sticking it out to the last and finishing with something in reserve."

The dogged Irish pack was thus born and it was a trait that has endured through the generations.

— LUCKY CHARM HONISS —

New Zealand referee Paul Honiss appeared to be Ireland's lucky charm for a period at the start of the millennium. The Kiwi presided over seven Irish wins out of seven up until February 2006.

Those games included victories over England at Twickenham in March 2004, over South Africa at Lansdowne Road in November 2004 and the memorable 27–25 win over France in Paris back in March 2000. Unfortunately, Honiss's streak came to an end at the Stade de France in 2006 when Ireland were thrashed 43–31 by France. Well, it was never going to last forever now, was it?

— BEFORE CONTACT LENSES —

Irish full-back Dolway Walkington, who earned eights caps for Ireland between 1887 and 1891, regularly wore a monocle because of his short-sightedness.

The NIFC player often tucked his monocle into his pocket before attempting a tackle, while in one famous incident against

Wales in 1891, he caught an up-and-under from a Welsh player, removed his monocle and then landed a beautiful drop goal.

Despite his intervention, Ireland lost the game at Stradey Park and Walkington never played for Ireland again.

— FIRST WINS —

Ireland played their first international on 15 February 1875, but it took six years and four days to record their first ever victory.

Scotland were the visitors to Belfast's Ormeau Road ground on that famous afternoon, and typical of the rugby of the day, it was an extremely tight affair. The game was scoreless at half-time but the Scots scored a soft try with five minutes to go to seemingly extend Ireland's miserable losing streak. But there was a twist in the tail. Back in the late 19th century, a try was worth one point, a drop goal three, and thus JC Bagot's late drop kick between the sticks snatched the game for the home side in the dying seconds.

Below is a list of Ireland's first victories over the major nations of world rugby and how long they took to achieve:

Team	First victory	Match number
Scotland	19 February 1891, Ormeau	4
England	5 February 1887, Lansdowne Road	13
Wales	3 March 1888, Lansdowne Road	4
France	20 March 1909, Lansdowne Road	1
Australia	19 January 1958, Lansdowne Road	3
South Africa	10 April 1965, Lansdowne Road	7
Italy	31 December 1988, Lansdowne Road	1
Argentina	31 August 1952, Buenos Aires	2

— PRE-MATCH LECTURE —

Hugo McNeill (1981–88) had a most unusual way of relieving tension in the build up to an international at Lansdowne Road.

The former Irish full back was a student of Anglo-Irish literature at Trinity College and on the Friday morning before Saturday tests, McNeill would take a stroll down to the College to take in a literature lecture from Brendan Kennelly, the popular Irish poet and novelist.

Having completed his studies in Dublin, McNeill went on to study at Oxford, playing in two varsity matches during his stay across the water.

— YOUNG MUNSTERS DENIED —

Young Munster are as proud a club as you'll find in Irish rugby and they almost had yet another remarkable tale to add to their rich history when Lansdowne Road played out its final games at the end of 2006.

Paul O'Connell, one of the Limerick club's most famous players, started things off by scoring the last try in the last international ever played at Lansdowne Road, against the Pacific Islands on 26 November.

A couple of weeks later Clem Casey, a former Young Munster player who switched allegiance to Lansdowne, scored the last try in the last club match at the ground for his new club.

All that was left was for a Young Munster associate to score the last try in the last interprovincial match played at the old venue, but unfortunately there wasn't one man with a connection to the club when Leinster met Ulster on New Year's Eve 2006.

For the record, Jamie Heaslip of Leinster scored the last interprovincial try at the Dublin 4 venue, the irony being that the number eight's father used to line out for Shannon during his playing days – Young Munster's arch rivals in Limerick.

— BLACKED OUT —

The All Blacks are the only team in international rugby that Ireland have played and never beaten. The countries have met on 20 occasions, with the All Blacks holding a record of 19 wins, one draw and no defeats. Below is Ireland's record of woe:

Date	Venue	Score
25 Nov 1905	Lansdowne Road	Ireland 0–15 All Blacks
1 Nov 1924	Lansdowne Road	Ireland 0–6 All Blacks
7 Dec 1934	Lansdowne Road	Ireland 9–17 All Blacks
9 Dec 1954	Lansdowne Road	Ireland 3–14 All Blacks
7 Dec 1963	Lansdowne Road	Ireland 5–6 All Blacks
20 Jan 1973	Lansdowne Road	Ireland 10–10 All Blacks
23 Nov 1974	Lansdowne Road	Ireland 6–15 All Blacks
5 June 1976	Athletic Park, Wellington	Ireland 3–11 All Blacks
4 Nov 1978	Lansdowne Road	Ireland 6–10 All Blacks
18 Nov 1989	Lansdowne Road	Ireland 6–23 All Blacks
30 May 1992	Carisbrook, Dunedin	Ireland 21–24 All Blacks
6 June 1992	Athletic Park, Wellington	Ireland 6–59 All Blacks
27 May 1995	Ellis Park, Johannesburg	Ireland 19–43 All Blacks
15 Nov 1997	Lansdowne Road	Ireland 16–63 All Blacks
17 Nov 2001	Lansdowne Road	Ireland 29–40 All Blacks
15 June 2002	Carisbrook, Dunedin	Ireland 6–15 All Blacks
22 June 2002	Eden Park, Auckland	Ireland 8–40 All Blacks
12 Nov 2005	Lansdowne Road	Ireland 7–45 All Blacks
10 June 2006	Waikato Stadium	Ireland 23–34 All Blacks
17 June 2006	Eden Park, Auckland	Ireland 17–27 All Blacks

— VICTOR BRAVO —

Former Leinster number eight Victor Costello, who earned 39 caps between 1996 and 2005, made his name in a different sporting arena before he came to prominence as a rugby player. Costello represented Ireland as a shot putter in the Barcelona Olympics in 1992 but he retired from the event immediately after the games, before making his mark with Leinster and his country.

— YOU STILL HERE? —

Mike Gibson and Tony O'Reilly share the record for the longest Ireland international careers. Both players wore the green jersey for 16 years, O'Reilly between 1954/55 and 1969/70 and Gibson between 1963/64 and 1978/79. Gibson, however, won the most caps of the durable twosome, the Ulsterman managing 60 appearances during his period at the top of the game as opposed to O'Reilly's 29.

— IRELAND BEAT THE BRITISH ARMY —

At the outbreak of the Second World War in 1939, all internationals were cancelled and Australia even had to return home without playing a match on disembarking from a two-month voyage from Sydney. The only release for rugby players were representative games against the armed forces and at Ravenhill in 1942 an Irish XV, which included would-be internationals, commenced a five game series against the British Army.

The Army won the first four games, all played in Belfast, with ease but the last of these fixtures, played at Ravenhill in December 1945, saw the Irish XV record their one and only win, by 19–3.

— PARC DES FARCE —

Between 1974 and 1996, Ireland lost 12 games in a row to France at the Parc des Princes in Paris. Ireland's luck in the French capital only changed when Les Bleus switched home venue to the Stade de France, with a Brian O'Driscoll hat-trick inspiring Ireland to a long-awaited 27–25 victory on 19 March 2000.

— RUGBY BY NUMBERS —

Ireland became the first team in world rugby to put numbers on their shirts when they took the field against England at Lansdowne Road in February 1926.

Ireland's innovation seemed to be something of a lucky omen, too, with the home side beating their close rivals 19–15. The rest of the Five Nations fastened onto the trend pretty rapidly but in England there was some variety on Ireland's innovation around the country. Leicester decided to use lettering instead of numbers, which flowed from A to O, from loose-head prop to full–back (with H being the openside flanker, G the number eight), while Bristol's similar alphabetic system went in the opposite direction, from O to A. As recently as 2006, the NSW Waratahs attempted to wear no numbers on their jerseys, just on their shorts, but were banned from doing so by the Super 14 committee.

— 2.4 MILLION EYES ON CROKE PARK —

The 2007 Six Nations encounter between Ireland and England at Croke Park is the most-watched rugby match in the history of Irish television. At its peak, an audience of 1.2million viewers tuned in to RTE 2 to watch Ireland's 43–13 victory, a figure that made it the most watched sports programme of the last ten years.

— IRISH LEGENDS: JACKIE KYLE —

Jackie Kyle, one of the game's great number tens

For many rugby aficionados out there, former Irish international Jackie Kyle is not only the best out-half to play for Ireland, he's also the best number ten ever to have graced the game. While comparisons of this nature, between the fully paid professionals of today and the amateurs of yesteryear, are always a little tenuous what we can say with complete certainty is that Kyle's abilities must have been pretty special to be remembered from an era where very little television footage exists.

Born in Belfast in 1910, Kyle studied medicine at Queens University but it was his prowess on the rugby pitch that marked him out from an early age. He made his debut as a 21-year-old in Ireland's first post-Second World War international against France in 1947, and it could be argued that he would have been wearing the green shirt a little sooner were it not for Europe's difficulties at the time.

The highlight of his career, like that of most of his team-mates, was the Grand Slam victory of 1948, the one and only time Ireland have achieved the feat. Kyle played in all four games that famous spring and his tactical abilities shone through like a beacon in an era when rugby teams got by without any formal coaching. Alongside team captain Karl Mullen, Kyle was the brains behind that legendary season, plotting Ireland's four superb victories to lead them to the promised land. The following year virtually the same side won the Triple Crown, but as many of the old legs headed into retirement, the out-half from Ulster continued for another eight years at the game's highest level.

Those who had the privilege of watching him play insist it was his patience that made Kyle the player he was. While he could punt to touch and hit a cross-field kick as well as any other kicking out-half at the time, Kyle had an unrivalled ability to beat a man if the opportunity arose. He would kick ball after ball down the field for the first half hour of a game and then, with the opposition lulled into a false sense of security, he'd then have a run at them, often with some success.

One solo try in particular, against France at Ravenhill, is still talked about to this day by those who witnessed it and it led to his French opponents christening him 'The Phantom', a nickname he's often reminded off when he visits that part of the world. Away from the Irish scene, Kyle also travelled on the 1950 Lions tour to New Zealand and Australia, playing in all six Tests in the southern hemisphere, and by the time he played his last game for Ireland against Scotland in March 1958, he had become Ireland's most capped player.

On retirement, Kyle got the travel bug and he first headed to

Indonesia to work as a doctor but left there after two years as the reign of President Sukarno turned nasty. Far from being deterred by this turn of events, he moved to Zambia (then North Rhodesia), to take up a post at Chigola Hospital, a job he stayed in until retiring in the summer of 2000. He now lives in Bryansford, south of Belfast.

Jackie Kyle
Born: 10 January 1926, Belfast
Clubs: Queens University and NIFC
Caps: 46
Scoring: 38 (7 tries, 1 drop goal)
Ireland debut: 25 January 1947 v France (Lansdowne Road)

— GEOGHEGAN'S CONDITION —

Irish winger Simon Geoghegan will forever be remembered as an exceptional speedster who had the misfortune of playing rugby in an era when Ireland rarely moved the ball past their centres.

But despite Ireland's conservatism at the time, the 37-times capped Londoner still managed to score 11 tries over the course of his career, a feat made all the more remarkable by his rare form of asthma. Geoghegan suffered from a condition termed 'exercise-induced asthma', a breathing difficulty that only came upon him during and after strenuous activity.

— O'GARA'S DOUBLE CELEBRATION —

Ronan O'Gara's try against France at Croke Park on 11 February 2007 was not only the first ever try scored by an Irishman at GAA headquarters, it was also the 100th try scored by Ireland in 81 fixtures against their Gallic cousins.

— THREE FOREIGN COACHES IN A ROW —

Murray Kidd, a New Zealander, became the first foreign coach of Ireland when he was appointed by the IRFU in the close season of 1995. The former Garryowen coach appeared out of his depth at rugby's top table and he was replaced in January 1997 by Englishman Brian Ashton. The former Bath coach appeared to have all the right credentials to become a success in his new job but after signing a six-year contract, he resigned before he was sacked following a defeat to Scotland in February 1998. Having clearly not tired of foreign coaches just yet, the IRFU decided to appoint then Connacht coach, and former All Blacks hooker, Warren Gatland to the position of head coach. The then 34-year-old steadied the ship impressively but he was sacked in November 2001 to be replaced by Eddie O'Sullivan.

Below are the records of Ireland's foreign coaches:

Coach	Won	Lost	Draw	Win %
Murray Kidd (1995–97)	3	6	0	33%
Brian Ashton (1997–98)	2	6	0	25%
Warren Gatland (1998–2001)	18	19	1	47%

— COME IN NUMBER 1000 —

Leinster's Jamie Heaslip became the 1,000th different player to earn an Irish cap when he made his international debut against the Pacific Islands on 26 November 2006. Three players – Stephen Ferris, Luke Fitzgerald and Heaslip – made their debuts on that day but Heaslip was deemed to be Ireland's 1,000th international because his name was called out second of the three by Eddie O'Sullivan when he officially named his team to play the Islanders.

— LET THERE BE LIGHT —

Floodlights were first installed at Lansdowne Road in 1995, primarily to allow the Irish football team to play midweek international matches at night.

The first international rugby match under lights at the venue was played on Tuesday 12 November 1996 but Murray Kidd, Irish coach at the time, probably wished someone could have switched them off halfway through the game. Ireland suffered an embarrassing 40–25 defeat to the Pacific Islanders and after another embarrassing defeat to Italy two months later, the coach was sacked.

— KIT SPONSORS —

Ireland have had two different shirt sponsors down the years, even if they've still managed to splash three different names across their shirts. In 1998 Irish Permanent, who then had Keith Wood on their staff, began their sponsorship of the Irish rugby team, a deal that continued when the financial institution changed its name to Permanent TSB back at the start of 2004. Then, at the end of the 2005/06 season, international mobile phone company, O2, signed a six-year deal with the IRFU, worth €9million, to have their name appear across Ireland's shirts.

— MERTHENS' MAGIC —

All Black Andrew Merthens holds the record for the most individual points in any game against Ireland. The out-half scored a tally of 33 points (a try, five conversions and six penalties) when New Zealand thrashed Ireland 63–15 at Lansdowne Road on 15 November 1997.

— EDDIE-ISMS —

Irish coach Eddie O'Sullivan is well known for his interesting sayings. Here are some of the most interesting 'Eddie-isms' that he has come out with over the years:

"You can't dwell on it, you can't unring a bell."

"Australia aren't all that and a bag of chips."

"Next weekend is going to be a tough one, whatever happened against New Zealand. Australia are going to be a different bag of hammers."

"We have to go at them like mad dogs in a meat house."

"It doesn't make the job any easier but it does mean if we get our ducks in a row, we can win it."

"If you are not locked and loaded, you'll get exposed and punished."

"If you expect us to win easily in Rome, you'd be whistling past a graveyard."

— STAN AWARDS ENGLAND'S POLDEN TRY —

Irish touch judge Stan Polden denied his own country a Triple Crown and Championship thanks to a controversial decision back in 1937.

After Ireland had beaten both Wales and Scotland in their opening championship fixtures, they headed off to play England at Twickenham with ambitions of something special. It looked like it might happen for a while too, with two tries from Fred Moran, an Irish sprint champion, earning the visitors a lead with just minutes to go. Then came Polden's intervention.

With the game almost up H.V. Sever, England's left-winger, motored down the touchline but he appeared to be bundled into touch by two covering Irish defenders just as he touched the ball down for a try.

The Welsh referee, J.W. Faull, was unable to decide whether Sever had scored the try so he consulted with Polden. To the cheers of the home crowd, Polden insisted that Sever had dotted the ball down before going into touch and the try was awarded. Victory, the Triple Crown and the Championship were England's, all thanks to an Irish official.

— BROTHERS IN ARMS —

Fifty sets of brothers have played for Ireland since the country's first fixture in 1875. The first band of brothers to play for Ireland in the same year were the three Ross brothers from Belfast, who earned international caps in 1886. The latest set of brothers to earn full Irish recognition were Guy and Simon Easterby.

— SWITCHING CODES —

After the celebrations of the 1948 Grand Slam were concluded, Ireland regrouped for the 1949 season short on numbers.

Two of their winning team, centre Paddy Reid from Limerick and Chris (or Jack as he was sometimes known)

Daly, a robust, athletic prop from Cobh, had accepted offers during the close season to switch codes and join the Huddersfield Rugby League side across the water in England. In Reid's case, it was a move of choice, and after a couple of months at Huddersfield, he was snapped up by Halifax. He was part of the team that lost the 1949 Challenge Cup final to Bradford Northern.

Daly, meanwhile, was somewhat forced into taking up Huddersfield's offer in the summer of 1948 for the simple reason that he was sacked from his job, and couldn't get another one, after celebrating a little too long following Ireland's Grand Slam-clinching victory over Wales. He too left Huddersfield after just one season, and went on to play for Featherstone Rovers. Like Reid, he also played in a Challenge Cup final, a defeat to Workington Town.

Other notable Irish players to switch codes down the years include Robin Thompson, a second row for Ulster who signed for Warrington after playing on the Lions tour of 1955 and Ken Goodall, another Ulster forward who joined Workington Town at the start of the 1970s.

— SCHOOLBOY DEBUT —

Frank Hewitt, a utility back from Instonians, is the youngest player to ever have played for Ireland. Hewitt made his Irish debut against Wales on 8 March 1924 aged 17 years and 157 days. He went on to earn nine international caps.

— MOST POINTS BY LIONS PLAYER IN A TEST MATCH —

Pts	Player	Opponents	Venue	Year
18	**Tony Ward**	**South Africa**	**Cape Town**	**1980**
18	Gavin Hastings	New Zealand	Christchurch	1993
17	**Tom Kiernan**	**South Africa**	**Pretoria**	**1968**

— BRAINS BEAT BRAWN —

The Irish Universities became the first ever Irish team to beat South Africa on 6 April 1965.

Captained by Jerry Walsh of UCC, a side missing Irish internationals Tom Kiernan, Pat McGrath, Ken Kennedy, Ray McLoughlin and Bill Mulcahy, defeated the Springboks 12–10 at Thomond Park. Tries from Eamonn McGuire and Mike Grimshaw, along with a Tony Hickie penalty and drop-goal from John Murray secured victory for the students in front of a raucous Limerick crowd.

Three days later Ireland defeated the Springboks 9–6 at Lansdowne Road, with Jerry Walsh once again playing his part in the defeat of the tourists.

— 85-SECOND CAP —

Sean McCahill is not only the holder of the shortest Irish international career, he's the holder of the second shortest career in international rugby.

McCahill, a New Zealand native, came onto the field as a substitute for one minute and 25 seconds of Ireland's game against Fiji at Lansdowne Road back in 1995.

Below are the other short-lived internationals:

Player	Match	Minutes on pitch
Nick Henderson	**Australia** v Pacific Islands (2004)	1min 02sec
Sean McCahill	**Ireland** v Fiji (1995)	1min 25sec
Mathieu Dourthe	**France** v New Zealand (2002)	2min
Mark Bartholomeusz	**Australia** v Italy (2002)	2min 33sec
Alexandre Albouy	**France** v Italy (2002)	2min 49sec

— IRELAND LEGENDS: MICK DOYLE —

Mick Doyle: player, coach, pundit

There aren't many international rugby players whose profiles increase after they hang up their boots but Mick Doyle, who passed away in 2004 at the age of 63, is remembered as much for his coaching abilities, and indeed his media punditry, as he is for his deeds on the rugby pitch.

It is a pity in a way because Doyle was a fine player, a

flanker who used his intelligence and never-say-die attitude to make up for his lack of physical stature. He first came to the attention of Irish selectors in 1965, while playing for University College Dublin during his veterinary studies at the Dublin university, making his international debut against France in a 3–3 draw at Lansdowne Road. He earned 20 caps before announcing his early and unexpected retirement from the international game in 1968. During that period on the international scene, he was never dropped for his country and this consistency and talent saw him selected for the 1968 Lions tour to South Africa.

With the international game behind him, Doyle completed his veterinary studies at Cambridge University – where he played in one varsity game – and he later went on to work alongside his father at his practice in Naas. Having disappeared from the rugby scene for a couple of years to concentrate on his business, Doyle re-emerged into the limelight in the late 1970s, coaching Leinster to five interprovincial titles in a row between 1979 and 1983. During his time with the province, they lost just one game out of 26 played and it was this superb record which landed him the job of Irish coach ahead of Willie John McBride for the 1984/85 season.

He proved an instant success in the job, leading Ireland to their first Triple Crown victory since 1948 within a couple of months of taking charge. The rugby his side played, particularly the side of 1985, was brave and fearless. Doyle wanted his players to "give it a lash" out on the field, asking them to run it and if that didn't work, run it some more. He was also way ahead of the field in terms of diet and nutrition, while his motivational qualities were also highly regarded by those who played under him. But despite all this, his Ireland side didn't achieve any more success under his tenure. At the inaugural 1987 World Cup in New Zealand and Australia, his side struggled badly, not helped by the heart attack Doyle suffered early in the tournament. He did, however, continue his role when released from hospital.

After the World Cup, Jim Davidson took over from Doyle

as Irish coach but his involvement in the game wasn't over quite yet. He started to write a column for both the *Evening Herald and Sunday Independent* newspapers and appeared on RTE television as a rugby pundit, invoking controversy at almost every turn.

Unlike many former players, Doyle wasn't afraid to shoot from the hip and his views both intrigued the public and annoyed the rugby hierarchy in equal measure. In 1996, he suffered a brain tumour and was lucky to escape with his life, the details of which were revealed in his excellent second book, *0.16 – Living in Extra Time*. He died in May 2004 in a car crash in Dungannon, leaving Irish rugby a much duller place.

Michael Gerard Martin Doyle
Born: 13 October 1941, Castleisland, Co Kerry
Clubs: UCD, Blackrock, Cambridge University, Edinburgh
Caps: 20
Scoring: 10 (2 tries)
Ireland debut: 23 January 1965 v France (Lansdowne Road)

— SCORELESS QUARTET —

From 11 February 1956 until 13 February 1960 Ireland were held scoreless by England on four consecutive occasions. The Irish scoring drought against the old enemy was finally broken at Twickenham in 1960 but Ireland didn't beat England again until the following year at Lansdowne Road, as they finally managed to break a run of five consecutive defeats. Below is the record of Ireland's scoreless run against England:

Date	Result	Venue
11 Feb 1956	Ireland 0–20 England	Twickenham
9 Feb 1957	Ireland 0–6 England	Lansdowne Road
8 Feb 1958	Ireland 0–6 England	Twickenham
14 Feb 1959	Ireland 0–3 England	Lansdowne Road

— IRELAND'S FIRST TOUR —

Twenty-four years after their first international, Ireland sailed to Canada in the summer of 1899 to undertake their first overseas tour. Just 17 players were selected to travel for the 11 matches in Canada and predictably enough for such a small party, Ireland were forced to play a number of games with just 14 men because of injuries.

Playing in such varied towns as Halifax, Montreal, Quebec, Toronto and Ottawa, Ireland won all but one of their fixtures, their only defeat coming against Nova Scotia early on in the tour. All costs on the trip were covered by Duke Collins, a Dublin native who lived in Toronto, but 'the Duke' had to cough up a little extra when J. Sproule Myles broke his leg in the early part of the tour. The player, who would later be elected a TD for East Donegal, was forced to stay in Canada a little longer than the rest of his team-mates (who arrived home in November) and he eventually set foot on Irish soil just in time for Christmas celebrations with his family.

— WEDDED BLISS —

Many Irish players have gone beyond the call of duty down the years but John Macauley from Limerick deserves special mention. The giant forward was so keen to get a day off work in order to play in Ireland's match against England at Lansdowne Road in 1887 that he got married on the morning of the game.

Macauley had already used up his holiday entitlement for the year by the time the match came around and the only way he could get another day off work was by getting hitched. Thankfully, his very understanding girlfriend didn't object to the idea and the forward's patriotic act was fully rewarded, with Ireland beating England for the first ever time after 12 previous unsuccessful attempts.

— WHAT THE TUCK? —

Ireland flanker Colm Tucker was at the centre of an unfortunate misprint in the match programme for the France and Ireland match at the Parc des Princes on 1 March 1980. Much to the amusement of his team-mates, the Shannon forward's surname was spelt with an 'F' instead of a 'T' in the team line-ups.

— BROTHERS IN ARMS —

Ireland fielded three sets of brothers against Wales at the Cardiff Arms Park in 1924. George and Harry Stephenson from Belfast, Dickie and Billy Collopy from Bective Rangers in Dublin and Frank and Tom Hewitt, also from Belfast, all played their part in Ireland's 13–10 victory, with the Hewitt brothers making history on the day in question by becoming the first brothers to score tries in an international game.

— LEADERS OF THE LIONS —

Ireland have provided more Lions captains, nine, than any other country. They are:

Player	**Tour**
Tom Smythe	South Africa, 1910
Sammy Walker	South Africa, 1938
Karl Mullen	New Zealand and Australia, 1950
Robin Thompson	South Africa, 1955
Ronnie Dawson	Australia and New Zealand, 1959
Tom Kiernan	South Africa, 1968
Willie John McBride	South Africa, 1974
Ciaran Fitzgerald	New Zealand, 1983
Brian O'Driscoll	New Zealand, 2005

— IRELAND'S MOST MEMORABLE TRIES: PAT CASEY V ENGLAND, 1964 —

13 February 1964 was the date, Twickenham the venue for what is now recognised, by general consensus, as Ireland's greatest ever try.

With Ireland leading England as the match headed into the last 15 minutes, Mike Gibson started the move that stunned those present at RFU headquarters. The Ulsterman made a clean break from just inside his own '25', as it was then, and transferred the ball inside to Jerry Walsh on a diagonal run, just inside the English half. With a couple of home defenders closing in on him, Walsh switched the direction of the attack for a second time and released Pat Casey on his inside. With England's chasers now completely flummoxed, the winger had the relatively simple task of dotting the ball down underneath the posts to give Ireland an 18–5 victory, their first win at Twickenham since the Grand Slam of 1948.

— IRELAND AT THE FIRST RUGBY WORLD CUP: 1987 —

Results and scorers
Pool 2

25 May	**Ireland** P: Kiernan (2)	**6–13 Wales**	Wellington
30 May	**Ireland** T: Crossan, McNeill, Spillane, Ringland, Bradley P: Kiernan (5) C: Kiernan (2)	**46–19 Canada**	Dunedin

3 June **Ireland** **32–9 Tonga** Brisbane
T: Mullin (3),
McNeill (2)
P: Ward (2)
C: Ward (3)

RWC Pool 2 Table

	P	W	D	L	F	A	PTS
Wales	3	3	0	0	82	31	6
Ireland	**3**	**2**	**0**	**1**	**84**	**41**	**4**
Canada	3	1	0	2	65	90	2
Tonga	3	0	0	3	29	98	0

Quarter-final
7 June **Ireland** **15–33 Australia** Sydney
T: Kiernan, McNeill
P: Kiernan
C: Kiernan (2)

Squad and Coach
Coach: Mick Doyle
Captain: Donal Lenihan

Forwards: W. Anderson (W, C, T, A), P. Collins (C), D. Fitzgerald (W, C, A), N. Francis (T, A), T. Kingston (W, C (r), T, A), J. Langbroek (T), D. Lenihan (W, C, T, A), J.J. McCoy (T), J. McDonald (C), D. McGrath (W, C, T, A), P. Matthews (W, T, A), P. Orr (W, C, A), B. Spillane (W, C, A (r))

Backs: M. Bradley (W, C, T, A), K. Crossan (W, C, T, A), P. Dean (W, A), D. Irwin (T, A, (r)), M. Kiernan (W, C, A), H. MacNeill (W, C, T, A) B. Mullin (W, C, T, A), T. Ringland (W, C, T, A), T. Ward (C, T)

Appearances as a replacement marked with (r)

— MOUTHING OFF —

"If Frankie Sheahan was playing 'William Tell', his son would have an arrow in his chest and not in his apple."
TV pundit George Hook after Ireland's defeat to Scotland in the foot-and-mouth international of 2001

"I may not have been very tall or very athletic, but the one thing I did have was the most effective backside in world rugby."
Former Irish second-row Jim Glennon gives away the secret to his rugby success in 1991

"Every time I went to tackle him, Horrocks went one way, Taylor the other and all I got was the bloody hyphen."
Mick English describes his attempts at getting his hands on English out-half Phil Horrocks-Taylor

"Tony Ward is the most important rugby player in Ireland. His legs are far more important to his country than even those of Marlene Dietrich were to the film industry. A little hairier, maybe, but a pair of absolute winners."
C.M.H. Gibson writes in the Wales v Ireland match programme from 1979

"Between us, me and my brother (Ray) have played 41 times for Ireland."
Irish prop Feidhlim McLoughlin fails to mention that he earned just the one cap

— FIRST IRISH SUBSTITUTE —

Mick Hipwell made Irish rugby history on 25 January 1969 when he became Ireland's first ever replacement. The Terenure College back row replaced the injured Noel Murphy in the game's second period, helping Ireland to close out a 17–9 win.

— IRELAND'S TRIPLE CROWNS: NO. 2, 1899 —

Ireland started their campaign with a win over England at Lansdowne Road, and they edged past Scotland in Murrayfield two weeks later to set up a Triple Crown and championship decider against Wales in Cardiff. Predictably, it was a nervy game with 'Blucher' Doran's try eventually proving the difference between the sides. Over the course of their Triple Crown winning season, only five Irish players started all three games, with 24 players being used in all by a selection committee who clearly didn't like their decisions to be predictable.

Date	Result	Venue
4 Feb 1899	Ireland 6–0 England	Lansdowne Road
18 Feb 1899	Ireland 9–3 Scotland	Inverleith
18 March 1899	Ireland 3–0 Wales	Cardiff Arms Park

— FIRST MAN OFF THE BENCH —

Irish international Barry Bresnihan became the first ever substitute in the whole of rugby union on the Lions tour of South Africa in 1968. The London Irish centre came on for fellow Irishman Mike Gibson in the tourists' opening fixture against Western Transvaal.

— NO SCORES ON THE DOORS —

Ireland have played in three scoreless matches in 132 years of international rugby:

Date	Result	Venue
18 Feb 1893	Ireland 0–0 Scotland	Ballynafeigh, Belfast
12 Feb 1910	Ireland 0–0 England	Twickenham
9 Feb 1963	Ireland 0–0 England	Lansdowne Road

— THIRD TIME LUCKY FOR O'CONNELL —

Paul O'Connell wanted to be a golf pro

Irish second-row Paul O'Connell had a go at two other sports before making it as a professional rugby player.

Between the ages of five and 14, O'Connell dedicated himself to swimming but when he realised he wasn't going to make it to the top of the sport, he switched tack to golf. Over a short period of time, O'Connell managed to reduce his handicap to six but when he couldn't get it any lower, he put all his time and energy into rugby with Ard Scoil Ris. Thankfully, his rapid rise through the Irish rugby ranks stopped him from switching sports again.

— TOURISTS GET THEIR COMMUPANCE —

On 18 January 1958, Irish rugby got another monkey off its back when Ireland defeated their first touring side. In almost 60 years of visits by travelling teams, which started with the New Zealand Maoris back in the 19th century, Ireland had never defeated a touring international side but that all changed when Australia came to visit Lansdowne Road. The game was Australia's third visit to Dublin and having won the first two fixtures between the sides, most observers predicated that the tourists would make it three in a row.

Noel Henderson's Ireland, however, were having none of it. A side that included the talents of David Hewitt, Gordon Wood, Noel Murphy, Bill Mulcahy and of course, Jackie Kyle, defeated Australia 9–6, the winning try being scored by the captain himself late on.

— ANYBODY GOT A LIGHT? —

Rob Henderson, who earned 29 caps between 1996 and 2003, will be remembered, among other things, for the hat-trick he scored against Italy in Ireland's 41–22 victory at Stadio Flaminio back in 2001.

Even more interesting than Henderson's tries that day was his admission afterwards that he played most of the game with a cigarette lighter in the pocket of his shorts having inadvertently brought it onto the field with him.

— IRFU PURCHASE LANSDOWNE ROAD —

Lansdowne Road hosted its first rugby international on 11 March 1878 against England but it wasn't until the early years of the next century that the IRFU actually purchased the ground.

Henry Wallace Doveton Dunlop initially leased the land in 1878 but as the years passed, Harry Sheppard, the honourary treasurer of the IRFU, took it off his hands. Although there was never any worry about using the ground while Sheppard had the lease in his possession, his sudden death in 1906 kicked the IRFU into action.

The Union offered the representatives of Sheppard's estate £200 for the lease, and with that piece of paper in their possession, they then went about securing the land on a more permanent basis from the Pembroke Estate. They initially signed a lease for 50 years at a fee of £50 per annum but in 1974 they finally purchased the freehold of the ground.

— BIG IN THE US —

Ireland posted their highest ever points tally and biggest margin of victory when they beat the USA 83–3 in New Hampshire in June 2000. The 13 tries scored that afternoon also represents the most tries Ireland have ever scored in an international. Below are the statistics from that triple record victory:

10 June 2000	**Ireland**	**83–3 USA**	New Hampshire
	T: S Easterby (2), Mullins (3) Murphy (2), G Easterby (2), O'Kelly, P Wallace, Humphreys, Topping C: O'Gara (8), Humphreys		

— NOT FURLONG —

Neville Furlong earned just two caps for his country but that didn't stop him making a name for himself.

Having shrugged off an ankle injury picked up in a warm-up match against Auckland, the winger made his international debut against the All Blacks at Carisbrook on 30 May 1992, a game which Ireland narrowly lost 24–21.

Despite exacerbating the injury during the game, Furlong was declared fit for the second test a week later in Wellington and he managed to hobble over the line for Ireland's only try in a 59–6 defeat. The try has gone down in history as Ireland's last four-pointer before the tally for a try was upped to five the following season but that's not his only claim to fame.

On return to Galway after the tour, Furlong was diagnosed with a broken bone in his ankle, making him not just the scorer of Ireland's last four-pointer, but also the country's first scorer of a try with a broken ankle.

— OH MY MY, JULY —

Ireland have only ever played two tests in the month of July. The first took place on 20 July 1991 in Windhoek where Ireland lost 15–6 to Namibia. Seven days later the tourists lost 26–15 to the rugby minnows in the same city.

— MOST PENALTIES —

Paul Burke holds the Irish record for most penalties scored in one game. The out-half, who played for Munster, Bristol, Harlequins and Leicester during his career, landed eight penalties against Italy at Lansdowne Road on 4 January 1997.

— SOUTH AFRICAN TOUR CONTROVERSY —

The Springboks' visit to Ireland in January 1970 was highly controversial, making front page news for the entire week before the test on the 10th of the month.

The anti-apartheid movement was the *cause célèbre* of the time, particularly because it was linked so closely with the civil rights crusade that was about to get into full swing in Northern Ireland. It appeared at one stage, before the South Africans arrived on Irish soil, that almost every trade union in the country would hinder the touring party in some way or other. Aer Lingus workers threatened not to handle the teams' baggage at Dublin airport. The General Workers' Union asked their members at the Royal Starlight Hotel in Bray, the Springbok base for their visit, not to prepare food for the rugby team. Even the postal unions got in on the act by telling its members not to assist with phone calls from the South African team hotel.

The most bizarre threat of all came from the IRA. The organisation issued a statement three days before the game promising to "take action" against the IRFU President and his committee if any protesters were hurt on the day of the game. As it was, few of the unions carried through with their threats but on the day of the game a crowd of 6,000 anti-apartheid protesters marched from O'Connell Street to Lansdowne Road in the presence of over 1,000 Gardai. There were fears that a certain section of the march would try to gain entry to the ground, but nothing untoward occurred when they reached Ballsbridge. Still, all the controversy in the week leading up the game caused the attendance to dip to below 30,000.

But everyone who went to the bother of turning up got their money's worth. The Springboks were coming to the end of an all-dominant era but they deserved to emerge from Lansdowne Road that afternoon as victors. A try from flanker Piet Greyling, and a penalty and conversion from full-back Henrie De Villiers gave the Boks their eight points, while an Alan Duggan try converted by Tom Kiernan meant that Ireland, miraculously, only trailed by three points as the referee started off into eight minutes of injury-time. With seven added minutes played, Ireland were awarded a penalty in front of the posts and Kiernan landed it to earn the draw.

— BEST OF THE WORST —

During the Five Nations Championship of 1981, Ireland lost all four of their matches, earning themselves the Wooden Spoon in the process, but their season wasn't as bad as it may seem. Tom Kiernan's side led each one of the four games at half-time and lost each of them by just a single score. Ireland's record that year was as follows:

Date	Result	Venue
7 Feb 1981	Ireland 13–19 France	Lansdowne Road
21 Feb 1981	Ireland 8–9 Wales	Cardiff Arms Park
7 March 1981	Ireland 6–10 England	Lansdowne Road
21 March 1981	Ireland 9–10 Scotland	Murrayfield

— NIGHT RUGBY —

Ireland's 1987 Rugby World Cup campaign was a bit of a farce, what with the team's lightweight performances on the pitch, the playing of the *Rose of Tralee* before the matches (see *God Save the Rose of Tralee*, page 11) and Mick Doyle's heart attack before the tournament even began.

In the midst of it all Donal Lenihan, Ireland's captain at the time, rang his mother to check how everything was at home. Talk eventually turned to Ireland's woes in New Zealand and Mrs Lenihan wasn't long in telling her son where Ireland were going wrong on the other side of the world.

"How do you expect to win if you go out and play rugby in the middle of the night," she said, as Donal nearly collapsed with laughter on the other end of the phone.

— IRISH LEGENDS: TOM CLIFFORD —

One story about Tom Clifford sums up the general esteem in which he was held in his native city. Long after he'd hung up his boots and was working as an aircraft refueller at Shannon Airport, the former Young Munster, Ireland and Lions prop used a bicycle as his main mode of transport around Limerick. The thing about Clifford's bike was that it never needed a lock. He could lay it up anywhere in the city and be confident that it would be there when he got back. Nobody would lay a finger on it.

The legend began when Clifford was just 14 years old. Young Munster were a man short for a game down in Cork against Constitution and they roped Clifford into playing full–back, despite his tender years. But even with this bright start to the adult game, his talent could almost have been lost on two fronts.

Clifford's skills as a soccer player were so good that he briefly flirted with a career in the sport with Limerick United in the League of Ireland before choosing rugby as his number one sport. And before that again, a bout of pleurisy which made him inactive for almost two years, threatened to halt his career before it even started. With the illness behind him, however, he graduated from full-back to the back-row once back on the rugby pitch until he eventually found his true calling as a loose-head prop.

Clifford made his Irish debut as a 26-year-old in the 1949 season – missing out on the Grand Slam by a season – but he did win a Triple Crown and Championship in his first year as a regular and a second Championship in 1951. His unremitting appetite for the physical side of the game, alongside his technical excellence in the frontrow, stood him apart from most of his contemporaries and he was selected to travel with the Lions on their 1950 tour of New Zealand and Australia. It was on this journey that the legend of Clifford truly flowered. First, there were the three trunks he brought with him for the journey. Most of his Lions colleagues thought

Clifford had brought a change of clothes for every day of the four-month tour but they soon found out that he was actually carrying a veritable larder of fruitcakes and biscuits baked by his mother. His cabin, unsurprisingly, soon became the epicentre of team activity on the voyage over, particularly after a few drinks had been downed.

Then, in New Zealand, Clifford showed the roguish side to his character. On the South Island, the Lions travelled by train to each match venue and when they arrived at every town on their itinerary, they marched behind a marching band, to the team hotel. Except for Clifford. He marched at the front, alongside the conductor. The band after all, he joked to his team-mates at the time, had come to greet him.

On that tour, Clifford played 19 of the 29 games, including five of the six Tests and although the Lions lost the series 3–0 in New Zealand, on his return Clifford was met by a marching band in Limerick, who guided him from the train station to a civic reception at the town hall. Eight thousand people marched behind him.

Clifford earned the last of his 14 Irish caps in 1952 against Wales and on his death in October 1990, Young Munster renamed their Greenfields ground 'Tom Clifford Park' where a huge portrait of the man himself now hangs in the main hall of the clubhouse.

Tom Clifford
Born: 15 November 1923, Co Tipperary
Club: Young Munster
Caps: 14
Scoring: 5 points (1 try)
Ireland debut: 29 January 1949 v France (Lansdowne Road)

— PIPPED AT THE POST —

Ireland's single point defeats through the years:

Date	Result	Venue
7 Feb 1885	Ireland 1–2 England	Manchester
21 Feb 1885	Ireland 0–1 Scotland	Ormeau, Belfast
6 Feb 1886	Ireland 0–1 England	Lansdowne Road
12 March 1887	Ireland 3–4 Wales	Birkenhead
11 Feb 1928	Ireland 6–7 England	Lansdowne Road
13 Feb 1937	Ireland 8–9 England	Twickenham
27 Feb 1960	Ireland 5–6 Scotland	Lansdowne Road
7 Dec 1963	Ireland 5–6 All Blacks	Lansdowne Road
1 March 1980	Ireland 18–19 France	Parc des Princes
21 Feb 1981	Ireland 8–9 Wales	Cardiff Arms Park
21 March 1981	Ireland 9–10 Scotland	Murrayfield
15 March 1986	Ireland 9–10 Scotland	Lansdowne Road
20 Oct 1991	Ireland 18–19 Australia	Lansdowne Road
18 Jan 1992	Ireland 15–16 Wales	Lansdowne Road
7 Feb 1998	Ireland 16–17 Scotland	Lansdowne Road
6 Feb 1999	Ireland 9–10 France	Lansdowne Road
1 Nov 2003	Ireland 16–17 Australia	Telstra Dome, Melbourne

— IRELAND'S MOST MEMORABLE TRIES: BRIAN O'DRISCOLL v FRANCE, 2000 —

"I was just in the right place at the right time," is how Brian O'Driscoll described the second of his three tries against France back in 2000 but he's being a bit modest.

The centre made inroads off scrum ball inside his own half and then offloaded to Girvan Dempsey on his inside. Then, in rapid succession, Anthony Foley, Denis Hickie and Simon Easterby brought Ireland deep inside the French 22. Peter Clohessy was halted just short with a carry around the fringes of a ruck but a couple of phases later and Malcolm O'Kelly fed O'Driscoll, who strolled over from five yards.

— BORN IN THE USA . . . AUSTRALIA, NEW ZEALAND —

While numerous players born in Britain have played for Ireland in the professional era, a handful of players born even further afield have donned the green jersey.

Player	**Born**
Isaac Boss	Tokoroa, New Zealand
Keith Gleeson	Sydney, Australia
Sean McCahill	Auckland, New Zealand
Matt Mostyn	Sydney, Australia
Mike Mullins	Auckland, New Zealand
Ross Nesdale	Feilding, New Zealand
Dion O'Cuinneagain	Cape Town, South Africa
Ronan O'Gara	San Diego, USA
Andy Ward	Whangrei, New Zealand

— IRELAND POACH MACLEAR —

On 11 February 1905, Cork hosted its first international fixture at the Mardyke, with England the visitors to the famous ground, but there was a more significant story on the day. Basil Maclear was an English soldier stationed in Fermoy at the time, but his visits home to play rugby were quite frequent and he came under the radar of the English selectors.

In January 1905, Maclear was playing in a club match for Old Bedfordians in front of an English selector and you'd imagine that the 11 tries and two goals he managed over the course of the game would make him a shoe-in for the Irish game. Not so. The selector stated that Maclear was "not good enough" and that the opposition weren't enough of a test of his true ability. On hearing this news, Ireland drafted Maclear into their starting line-up for the game against England and the centre enjoyed an outstanding match in what was at the time a rare Irish victory.

— EVITA PUTS TOUR IN JEOPARDY —

The Argentinean leg of Ireland's summer tour to South America in 1952 was nearly called off because of the death of Eva Peron.

Argentina's First Lady died on 26 July in Buenos Aires, six days after the Irish squad and officials had departed Dublin for the first leg of their tour in Chile. The tourists' first match was against the Chilean All Stars in Santiago but as they began their journey to Buenos Aires soon after beating the home side 30–0, there was still some doubt as to whether their games against the Pumas would actually take place, such was the outpouring of grief at Peron's death. In the end the rugby went ahead, with Ireland winning one and drawing the other of their two test matches against a surprisingly powerful Argentinean outfit.

Overall, Des O'Brien's Ireland won six, drew two and lost one of their nine tour games in South America.

Result	**Venue**	
Ireland 30–0	Chilean All Starts	Santiago
Ireland 12–6	Capital	Buenos Aires
Ireland 6–11	Pucara	Buenos Aires
Ireland 6–6	Buenos Aires XV	Buenos Aires
Ireland 19–3	Argentina 'A'	Buenos Aires
Ireland 3–3	Argentina	Buenos Aires
Ireland 25–3	Argentina 'B'	Buenos Aires
Ireland 6–0	Argentina	Buenos Aires
Ireland 19–11	Argentina Uni	Buenos Aires

— MISSING LETTERS —

No player with a surname beginning with 'V', 'X' or 'Z' has ever represented Ireland at international level. The letter 'U' has just the one international, Hex Uprichard who earned two caps back in 1950. The letter 'Y' has four internationals, while 'I' has five.

— QUICK STAND —

There was no messing about when the IRFU bought land at Ravenhill, Belfast in 1923. The Ormeau Grounds had been Ulster's venue of choice since they played their first interprovincial match against Leinster back in 1875, but once the decision was taken to buy a new patch of land for rugby purposes, a main stand and terracing on all four sides was erected in just 300 days.

The land itself was bought for the sum of £2,300 and the Union paid £15,500 to get their rapid fire work completed. The first international was played at the new venue the following year, with visitors England beating the home side 14–3. Since then, Ravenhill has hosted 16 Irish internationals, including the World Cup warm-up game against Italy in August 2007.

— IRELAND AT THE SECOND RUGBY WORLD CUP: 1991 —

Results and scorers
Pool 2

6 Oct	**Ireland**	**55–11 Zimbabwe**	Lansdowne Road
	T: Curtis, Geoghegan Popplewell (2), Robinson (4) P: Keyes (5) C: Keyes (4)		
9 Oct	**Ireland**	**32–16 Japan**	Lansdowne Road
	T: Mannion, O'Hara, Staples, P: Keyes (4) C: Keyes (2)		
12 Oct	**Ireland**	**15–24 Scotland**	Edinburgh
	P: Keyes (4) DG: Keyes		

RWC Pool 2 Table

	P	W	D	L	F	A	PTS
Scotland	3	3	0	0	122	36	9
Ireland	**3**	**2**	**0**	**1**	**102**	**51**	**7**
Japan	3	1	0	2	77	87	5
Zimbabwe	3	0	0	3	31	158	3

Quarter-final

20 Oct **Ireland 18–19 Australia** Lansdowne Road
T: Hamilton
P: Keyes (3)
C: Keyes

Squad and Coach

Coach: Ciaran Fitzgerald
Captain: Philip Matthews

Forwards: D. Fitzgerald (Z, S, A), G. Hamilton (Z, J, S, A), N. Francis (Z, J, S, A), D. Lenihan (Z, S, A), M. Galwey (J), N. Mannion (J), P. Matthews (Z, S, A), P. O'Hara (J), N. Popplewell (Z, S, A), B. Robinson (Z, S, A) S. Smith (Z, S, A)

Backs: J. Clarke (J, A), K. Crossan (Z, J, A), V. Cunningham (Z, J (r)), D. Curtis (Z, J, S, A), S. Geoghegan (Z, S, A), R. Keyes (Z, J, S, A), B. Mullin (J, S, A) R. Saunders (Z, J, S, A), J. Staples (Z, J, S, A)

Appearances as a replacement marked with (r)

— ACROSS CODES —

Brian Carney made history on 26 May 2007 when he became the first player in Irish rugby history to earn a full international cap having crossed codes from Rugby League to Rugby Union. Before converting to Union in the early months of that same year, Carney played with the Great Britain and Ireland Rugby League team, having played his club rugby with Wigan in England and the Gold Coast Titans in Australia.

— WINNING STREAK —

Ireland's longest winning sequence spanned ten matches between September 2002 and March 2003. The run started with a victory over Romania in Limerick and came to a halt when England won the Grand Slam at Lansdowne Road on 30th March 2003. Below is a full list of Ireland's historic winning sequence:

Date	Result	Venue
7 Sept 2002	Ireland 39–8 Romania	Thomond Park
21 Sept 2002	Ireland 35–3 Russia	Krasnoyarsk
28 Sept 2002	Ireland 63–14 Georgia	Lansdowne Road
9 Nov 2002	Ireland 18–9 Australia	Lansdowne Road
17 Nov 2002	Ireland 64–17 Fiji	Lansdowne Road
23 Nov 2002	Ireland 16–7 Argentina	Lansdowne Road
16 Feb 2003	Ireland 36–6 Scotland	Murrayfield
22 Feb 2003	Ireland 37–13 Italy	Stadio Flaminio
8 March 2003	Ireland 15–12 France	Rome
22 March 2003	Ireland 25–24 Wales	Millennium Stadium

— SHIRTS ON THEIR BACKS —

Ireland wore green-and-white hooped shirts for their first ever international against England at the Oval in 1875. The ensemble was completed with white shorts and green-and-white hooped socks. For their second game, against England at Rathmines later that same year, Ireland wore white shirts with a shamrock crest, along with navy blue shorts and blue stockings. The green shirt with the shamrock crest was first worn the next season and has been used by Ireland ever since.

— IRELAND'S TRIPLE CROWNS: NO. 3, 1948 —

The 1948 Grand Slam Team

Not only was this Ireland's third Triple Crown, it also represented their first ever Grand Slam. Karl Mullen's side stormed through the early games of their campaign, beating France, England and Scotland in a series of tight encounters, leaving their old bogey side, Wales, standing between them and their third Triple Crown and first Grand Slam title. The force was with Ireland, however, and in an extremely tough game – captain Karl Mullen had a pair of black eyes by the end – tries by Chris Daly and Barney Mullan were enough to give Ireland the first Triple Crown victory in 49 long, and also, their one and only Grand Slam to date.

Date	Result	Venue
1 Jan 1948	Ireland 13–6 France	Stade Colombes
14 Feb 1948	Ireland 11–10 England	Twickenham
28 Feb 1948	Ireland 6–0 Scotland	Lansdowne Road
13 March 1948	Ireland 6–3 Wales	Ravenhill

— DROP GOAL KING —

Ronan O'Gara leads the list of Ireland's drop goal kings:

Drops	Player	Caps	Career
10	Ronan O'Gara	73	2000–
8	David Humphreys	72	1996–2005
7	Richard Lloyd	19	1910–1920
7	Ollie Campbell	22	1976–1984
6	Mike Gibson	69	1964–1979
6	Barry McGann	25	1969–1976
6	Michael Kiernan	43	1982–1991

— DOUBLE TAKE —

Irish internationals with the exact same name and spelling:

Name	Caps	Career	Caps	Career
William Brown	1	1899	4	1970
William Collis	7	1924–26	1	1884
John Fitzgerald	12	1988–94	1	1884
Michael Gibson	10	1979–88	69	1964–79
Denis Hickie	58	1997–	6	1971–72
Ted McCarthy	1	1898	1	1892
John Murphy (x3)	1	1993	6	1951–58
	3	1981–84		
Noel Murphy	11	1930–33	41	1958–69
Jack O'Connor	1	1895	1	1909
James Stevenson	2	1888–89	5	1958

— IRISH LEGENDS: OLLIE CAMPBELL —

Ollie Campbell did the basics brilliantly

The greatest pity about Ollie Campbell's career is not that he earned just the 22 caps in eight years of international rugby, but that his significant deeds on the pitch will always be secondary in the eyes of most rugby supporters to his longstanding battle for the Irish number ten shirt with Tony Ward. In the late 1970s and early 1980s, the players fought out a manful battle for the right to be Ireland's first choice out-half, and if neither of them really won the scrap, it could be said with some authority that Campbell was always the selectors' default choice when things weren't going well.

All of which suggests that Campbell was a safe pair of hands, a conservative who did the basics well, but that description does an incredible disservice to his wide range of talents. A kicker of some renown, be that with the dead ball or out of hand, Campbell could break and pass as least as good as most out-halves of the era but he rarely received the full credit he deserved for those particular aspects of his game.

A student of Old Belvedere College in North Dublin, Campbell made his Irish debut as a 22-year-old in January 1976 against Australia at Lansdowne Road but just as he settled in for a sustained spell as Ireland's number ten, Tony Ward arrived on the scene. The Munster out-half was selected for Ireland for the duration of the 1978 and 1979 seasons and Campbell only fully regained his place on Ireland's victorious summer tour to Australia in 1979, where he played an instrumental part in his side's 2–0 victory over the home side. The Ward saga would continue until Campbell announced his retirement in 1984 but to concentrate too much on that ding-dong battle would be completely unfair on the Old Belvedere player's achievements.

For one, he was selected to tour South Africa with the Lions in 1980, a series during which he came on as a replacement in the second game, and started the third and fourth Tests, as the Lions went down 3–1 to the Springboks. Three years later, Campbell was the first choice out-half on the Lions' ill-fated tour of New Zealand, starting all of the Tests as the tourists went down to a 4–0 whitewash.

Still, that tour was more than just a trip for Campbell, who had been completely besotted by New Zealand and more particularly, the All Blacks, from an early age. The player himself has admitted that of over 200 rugby books he has on his shelves, at least 90% of them concern the All Blacks and while many of the players on that particular tour enjoyed very little of it, Campbell was in awe at playing in places like Pukekohe, Invercargill, Wellington, Auckland, Dunedin and the like.

But it was before that tour that Campbell enjoyed his most prolific spell in an Irish shirt. Under the guidance of Tom Kiernan, Ireland won a Triple Crown in 1982 and it would have been a Grand Slam had the break between the Scottish and French games not been four weeks long. As it was, Campbell's performance in scoring all 21 Irish points in their Triple Crown-winning game against Scotland at Lansdowne Road that season has gone down as one of the greatest ever Irish virtuoso performances.

Campbell retired from the international game at the end of the 1984 season because of chronic hamstring problems and he now works for the Eastern Health Board in Dublin.

Ollie Campbell
Born: 5 March 1954, Dublin
Club: Old Belvedere
Caps: 22
Scoring: 218 points (1 try, 54 pens, 15 cons, 7 dgs)
Ireland debut: 17 January 1976 v Australia (Lansdowne Road)

— OVER OR OUT? —

Before Ireland recorded their first win over England in 1887 they were involved in a controversial incident that denied them a famous victory.

In the final minutes of the game between the sides at Lansdowne Road on 5 February 1881, Meredith Johnston crossed for a late try to draw Ireland level with their opponents. Naturally enough, Johnston's effort gave Robert McLean the opportunity to win the game for his side with the conversion but that was only the start of the drama late in the game. McLean made a solid connection with his kick and was given a raised flag by one touch judge. The trouble was his colleague didn't agree with him and the conversion wasn't awarded, denying the Irish players on the day a piece of history.

IRELAND SHIRTS
1875–2009

1875 v England

1875 v England

1876-1995

1995-97

1995 World Cup

1997-99

1997-99

1999 World Cup

1999-2000

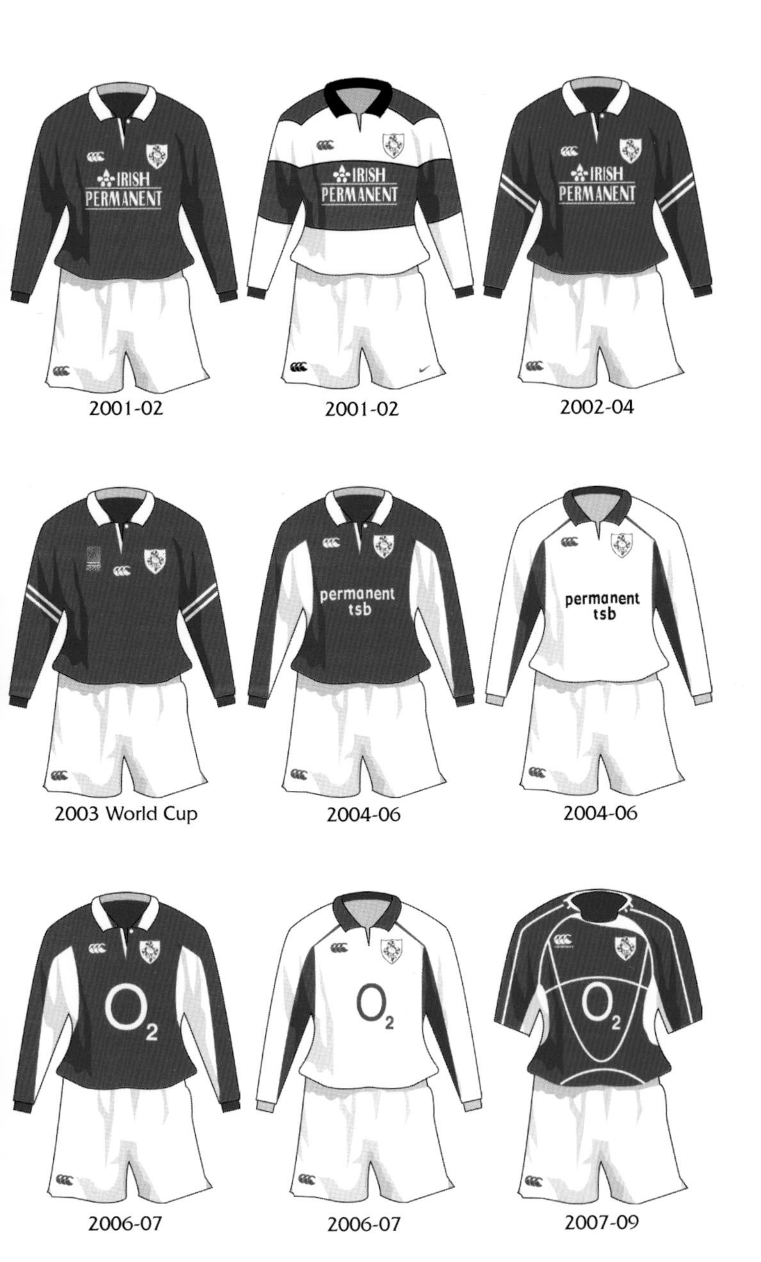
IRISH
PERMANENT
2001-02
IRISH
PERMANENT
2001-02
IRISH
PERMANENT
2002-04
2003 World Cup
permanent
tsb
2004-06
permanent
tsb
2004-06
O2
2006-07
O2
2006-07
O2
2007-09

2007-09

2007 World Cup

2007 World Cup

WWW.CAKEBREADILLUSTRATIONS.COM

— IRELAND'S TRIPLE CROWNS: NO. 4, 1949 —

An opening day defeat to France put paid to all hopes of a second successive Irish Grand Slam but a couple of victories over England at Lansdowne Road and Scotland at Murrayfield set Ireland up for another Triple Crown attempt. Once again, Wales were standing in their way and it proved to be yet another nerve-wracking day. Following a tetchy first period, a try from flanker Jimmy McCarthy, converted by George Norton, gave Ireland their fourth Triple Crown success and results elsewhere ensured that they claimed the Championship outright too.

Date	Result	Venue
29 Jan 1949	Ireland 9–16 France	Lansdowne Road
12 Feb 1949	Ireland 14–5 England	Lansdowne Road
26 Feb 1949	Ireland 13–3 Scotland	Murrayfield
12 March 1949	Ireland 5–0 Wales	Swansea

— WAITING ROOM —

Tony O'Reilly and Jim Glennon hold the dubious honour of having had to wait the longest period between Irish caps.

O'Reilly earned his 28th Irish cap against Wales on 9 March 1963 but he had to wait until 14 February 1970 – a period of almost seven years – to win cap number 29 against England at Twickenham. O'Reilly was 33 years old when he won his final cap, one year younger than Glennon was when he returned from international exile.

The Leinster second-row earned his second Irish cap against Scotland on 2nd February 1980 but number three didn't arrive until 7th February 1987 when he took the field against England at Lansdowne Road.

— ANDERSON AND ARGENTINA —

Irish second-row Willie Anderson (1984–90) nearly sparked an international incident when facing the New Zealand Haka at Lansdowne Road in 1989 (see *Willie or Won't He?*, page 9), but nine years previously the Ulster man did start a genuine diplomatic episode while on tour with The Penguins (a representative touring side) in Argentina.

It all started when Anderson took a liking to the Argentinean flag hanging outside his hotel and decided he'd quite like to bring it home with him as a souvenir. Minutes after he took the flag, six men with machine guns burst into his room looking for the missing flag and even though Anderson handed it back and apologised for taking it, he was taken to a police station that evening with fellow Irish internationals David Irwin and Frank Wilson. After being interrogated for a number of hours, Anderson was then brought to court where the charges were levelled against him.

Three weeks after the incident Irwin and Wilson – whose only role in the whole affair was accompanying Anderson to the police station – were released without charge but the big second-row had to stay a further two months in Argentina until his trial. Anderson was subsequently cleared of the charges but only after spending £10,000 on legal fees to clear his name.

— THE FOUR TRY CLUB —

Irish players who have scored four tries in a test match:

Player	Date	Opponents	Venue
Brian Robinson	6 Oct 1991	Zimbabwe	Lansdowne Road
Keith Wood	2 Oct 1999	United States	Lansdowne Road
Denis Hickie	20 Aug 2003	Italy	Thomond Park

— MUNSTER AND THE TOURISTS —

Munster have always relished their games against international touring sides and they've claimed a few memorable scalps, as well as administering a fair few frights, in both Limerick and Cork over the past century or so. They lost 6–5 to a last-minute try against Australia back in 1947, the All Blacks managed to eek out a 6–3 victory in Limerick in 1963 but their first major shock came at Musgrave Park against Australia on 25 January 1967. A John Moroney try, converted by Tom Kiernan put Munster in the ascendancy and with the full-back knocking over a further two penalties on the day, the home side went on to record a much deserved 11–8 victory.

In 1973 the All Blacks were held 3–3 in Cork, a last-minute penalty from visiting out-half Trevor Morris saving his side's blushes. That same year, Munster drew 12–12 with Argentina in a bad-tempered game at Thomond Park, while in 1976 Australia just about avenged their 1967 defeat with a 15–13 win at Musgrave Park.

Then came Munster's greatest day, their 12–0 drubbing of the All Blacks on 31 October 1978. A hundred thousand people, at the very least, claim to have been there in the flesh but in fact the real figure was somewhere in the region of 12,000, all of whom witnessed Seamus Dennison scoring a try, Tony Ward converting it and the out-half also knocking over two drop goals to seal a most famous victory.

Since that All Blacks game, Munster have gone on to beat the Wallabies on two further occasions, a 15–6 victory at Thomond Park in 1981 and a memorable 22–19 victory at Musgrave Park 11 years later, courtesy of a late Jim Galvin drop goal.

— ON A PRAYER —

Father Tom Gavin of London Irish became the first, and indeed last, Catholic priest to play for Ireland when he was capped in the centre against France at Lansdowne Road on 29 January 1949 – a Sunday incidentally – and earned a second cap two weeks later against England at the same venue. Gavin, then 26, was dropped for Ireland's next game against Scotland and was never capped again.

— DURACELL BUNNIES —

The Irish internationals to have played the most consecutive tests:

Tests	Player	Span
52	Willie John McBride	1964–1975
49	Phil Orr	1976–1986
43	Donal Lenihan	1981–1989
39	Moss Keane	1974–1971
37	George Stephenson	1920–1929

— IRELAND'S FIRST CAPTAIN —

George Stack had the honour of captaining Ireland in their first ever international game, against England on 15 February 1875, but the Trinity College player did a lot more besides leading his team onto the field.

The very first meeting of the Irish Football Union (IFU), one of the IRFU's predecessors, took place in Stack's rooms at Trinity in December 1874 and he was then heavily involved in making the arrangements for that first game against England at the Oval.

The defeat in London proved to be Stack's only Irish cap and he died unexpectedly in tragic and suspicious circumstances in November 1876, a year and half after his greatest honour.

— JAMES CECIL PARK —

Irish international James Cecil Parks was quite the tennis player. A talented back on the rugby pitch, Parks also represented his country in the Davis Cup and the 1908 Olympic Games, while he won also won three Mixed Doubles titles at Wimbledon.

— ROG AND THE DOLPHINS —

Ronan O'Gara was headhunted as a kicker by the Miami Dolphins during the 2002/03 season.

The Irish out-half admitted to having had an informal conversation with an agent representing the Miami Dolphins but that was as far as the story went, even if it did receive widespread media coverage at the time. Some reports suggested that O'Gara had been offered $100,000 a week to sign for the American football side but the Munster man was quick to put the rumours to bed.

— FULL HOUSE OF CAPS —

Jeremy Staunton and Donncha O'Callaghan are the only two Irish player to have been capped at every possible grade from Schools or Youth level upwards.

The players, who both started their careers with Munster, have represented Ireland at Schools/Youths, Under-19, Under-21, Under-25, Students, 'A' and Full Senior level over the past decade or so. Paddy Johns of Ulster and Jack Clarke of Munster missed out getting the full house by not being capped at Under-19 level, while Leo Cullen and Bob Casey never played for the Irish Universities side.

— MOST POINTS IN A MATCH BY A PLAYER —

Mr Reliable: Ronan O'Gara

The Irish players who have scored the most points in a single game:

Pts	Player	Date	Opp	Venue
32	Ronan O'Gara	20 June 2003	Samoa	Apia
30	Ronan O'Gara	4 March 2000	Italy	Lansdowne Road
26	David Humphreys	16 Feb 2003	Scotland	Murrayfield

26	David Humphreys	30 Aug 2003	Italy	Limerick
24	Paul Burke	4 Jan 1997	Italy	Lansdowne Road
24	David Humphreys	20 Oct 1999	Argentina	Lens
23	Ralph Keyes	6 Oct 1991	Zimbabwe	Lansdowne Road
23	Ronan O'Gara	11 Nov 2000	Japan	Lansdowne Road
22	David Humphreys	3 Feb 2002	Wales	Lansdowne Road

— WHITEWASHES —

Ireland's Five Nations whitewashes down the years:

Year	Results
1884	England 3–0; Scotland 8–1; Wales 5–0
1891	England 9–0; Scotland; 14–0; Wales 6–4
1895	England 6–3; Scotland 6–0; Wales 5–3
1909	England 11–5; Scotland 9–3; Wales 18–5
1920	England 14–11; Scotland 19–0; Wales 28–4; France 15–7
1934	England 13–3; Scotland 16–9; Wales 13–0
1938	England 36–14; Scotland 23–14; Wales 11–5
1960	England 8–5; Scotland 6–5; Wales 10–9; France 23–6
1977	England 4–0; Scotland 21–18; Wales 25–9; France 15–6
1981	England 10–6; Scotland 10–9; Wales 9–8; France 19–13
1984	England 12–9; Scotland 32–9; Wales 18–9; France 25–12
1986	England 25–20; Scotland 10–9; Wales 19–12; France 29–9
1992	England 38–9; Scotland 18–10; Wales 16–15; France 44–12
1998	England 35–17; Scotland 17–16; Wales 30–21; France 18–16

— THE GARRYOWEN —

Garryowen RFC, founded in 1884, are in the unique position of having an element of the sport named after them. In their early years, the Limerick club used the up-and-under so much as a tactic in their games, that it soon became known as a 'garryowen' in and around the rugby-mad city. The term then spread across the Irish rugby scene and is now accepted rugby parlance anywhere in the world.

— SEEING RED —

Willie Duggan (1975–84) became the first Irish player ever to be sent of in a full international on 15th January 1977. Duggan was sent off for fighting during his side's 25–9 defeat to Wales at Cardiff Arms Park but the blow of the Irish forward's dismissal was softened somewhat by the fact that Wales's Geoff Wheel was also sent to the dressing-room for his involvement in the same altercation.

— LOST IN BATTLE —

Almost a quarter of all Irish players belong to the one-cap wonder club and while some have tales of woe as to why they never made it to two, the story of Jasper Brett is undoubtedly the cruellest of them all.

The 18-year-old wing from Monkstown made his international debut against Wales on 14 March 1914, a game that proved to be Ireland's last fixture before the start of the First World War. Brett, like many young Irish rugby players at the time, was drafted into the British Army early the next year and was killed on the battlefields of Europe within six months of leaving home, cutting a promising life and rugby career tragically short.

— KEEP THE FLAG FLYING —

The Irish tricolour went missing from international matches at Lansdowne Road in the late 1920s and early 1930s, in an attempt to stop the political changes in the country from inflicting upon rugby.

Following the formation of the Irish Free State in 1922 and Ireland's independence from Britain, the IRFU decided to come up with their own flag (the crests of the four provinces in each corner on a green background) in order to stop any potential disagreements before they started.

The plan was to fly the new flag at both Lansdowne Road and Ravenhill in place of the Irish and British flags during international fixtures but things were never likely to be as simple as that.

While the British flag ceased to be flown at Ravenhill after 1925, the Connacht Branch raised the issue of the Tricolour at Lansdowne Road on numerous occasions with the IRFU over the coming years. Their persistence eventually paid off. In 1932, the Minister for External Affairs in the Free State Government met the Union President on the matter. After the meeting, it was decided that the national flag would be flown alongside the IRFU's own concoction at all Lansdowne Road games, a protocol that has been observed ever since.

— IRELAND'S ALL TIME TOP POINTS SCORERS —

Pts	Player	Tests	Career
760	Ronan O'Gara	73	2000–
560	David Humphreys	72	1996–2005
308	Michael Kiernan	43	1982–1991
296	Eric Elwood	35	1993–1999
217	Ollie Campbell	22	1976–1984
158	Tom Kiernan	54	1960–1973
152	Brian O'Driscoll	68	1999–
125	Denis Hickie	52	1997–2005
113	Tony Ward	19	1978–1987

— IRISH LEGENDS: KARL MULLEN —

Karl Mullen has gone down in the history books as the most successful Irish captain of all time. Under the hooker's inspirational leadership, Ireland won their one and only Grand Slam in 1948, as well as a Triple Crown and Championship in 1949 and the Championship all on its own in 1951. That period still represents Ireland's most prolific era but the one pity is that it didn't begin sooner.

Mullen made his full Irish debut in 1947 against France at Lansdowne Road, but he had been playing since 1945 in various Irish selections against representative sides from across Britain. When international rugby fully resumed after the Second World War, however, Mullen went about making up for lost time. After taking the captain's armband from Ernie Strathdee following the opening match against France in 1948, the hooker went about putting his stamp on the Irish team. Mullen's abilities as a leader, or as a coach as he effectively was, not only centred on defining how his side would play but also in pinpointing weaknesses in the opposition. In an era without video footage, Mullen along with his tactical sidekick Jackie Kyle, were able to decide within a couple of minutes of a game starting how best to deal with the opposition.

During the interval in the Grand Slam decider against Wales that year, Mullen proved his abilities as a leader by asking Jimmy Nelson to do a job on Welsh second-row Rhys Stephens, who had lorded proceedings in the first-half. Nelson snuffed out Stephens' threat and Chris Daly's second-half try earned Mullen's side their piece of history.

The following season, Mullen continued as captain and only a defeat to France in Ireland's first game denied his side a second Grand Slam. In the Five Nations Championship of 1950, Mullen once again led by example but despite losing to both England and France, the hooker was selected to lead the Lions summer tour to New Zealand. Eight of his fellow Irishmen accompanied him on the arduous trip by boat and things were hardly easier when they reached dry land. Mullen's side lost three of their four Tests against the All Blacks, drawing the other, but the captain did miss the final two Tests after pulling a muscle in his leg during training.

On his return, Mullen was as keen as ever to achieve Irish success but his side, which had been almost completely restructured since 1948, missed out on a second Grand Slam by virtue of a 3–3 draw against Wales on the last day of the Championship. He soldiered on for one more season, but success once again just eluded Ireland as they missed out on the Triple Crown victory thanks to a final day defeat to England.

On retirement from the game, Mullen established himself as a well respected doctor having earned a medical degree from UCD during his playing days.

Karl Mullen
Born: 26 November 1926, Wexford
Club: Old Belvedere
Caps: 25
Scoring: 0
Ireland debut: 25 January 1947 v France (Lansdowne Road)

— BENCH SPLINTERS —

David Humphreys holds the record for the most appearances as an Irish substitute. The Ulster out-half has come onto the field as a replacement for Ireland on 28 separate occasions. Below is the list of Ireland's top substitutes:

Sub apps	Player	Career
28	David Humphreys	1996–
21	Guy Easterby	2000–2005
18	Marcus Horan	2000–
18	Donncha O'Callaghan	2003–
17	Frankie Sheahan	2000–
16	Ronan O'Gara	2000–

— TICKETS PLEASE —

The first all-ticket match in the history of international rugby was between Ireland and the All Blacks at Lansdowne Road in 1905.

Dave Gallaher's 'Invincibles' beat Ireland 15–0 on 1 November, despite a brave effort from a home side clearly out of their depth. Ireland were probably even prouder of their efforts in that fixture by the time the All Blacks finished their tour a couple of months later. Gallaher's side beat Wales 19–0, England 17–9 and France 30–6 over the course of the rest of their mammoth tour and by the time they returned to their homeland in the early months of 1925, they had posted an incredible record of 32 wins from 32 games.

— IRELAND AND THE PROFESSIONAL ERA —

Although, Ireland played their first game of the professional era on 18 November 1995 against Fiji at Lansdowne Road, it would not be totally correct to state that the Irish side were fully professional at the time. The players who took to the field that day were paid for their troubles, but most still held down full-time jobs and it wasn't until a number of years later that Irish rugby became fully professional.

Date	Progress
1995/96	International players paid per game but no formal contract
1996/97	34 full-time players are contracted centrally by the IRFU
1997/98	Provinces allowed to contract 10 full-time players and 20 part-time
1998/99	Provinces allowed to contract 21 full-time players plus part-timers
1999/00	Provinces allowed to contract 30 full-time players

— LIST OF FOES —

A list of all Ireland's opponents in international matches and their record against each:

Opponent	P	W	D	L
Argentina	9	5	0	4
Australia	26	8	0	18
Canada	3	2	1	0
England	120	43	8	69
Fiji	2	2	0	0
France	81	28	5	48
Georgia	2	2	0	0
Italy	15	12	0	3
Japan	5	5	0	0
Namibia	3	1	0	2
New Zealand	20	0	1	19
Pacific Islands	1	1	0	0
Romania	8	8	0	0
Russia	1	1	0	0
Samoa	4	3	0	1
Scotland	120	53	5	62
South Africa	18	3	1	14
Tonga	2	2	0	0
United States	5	5	0	0
Wales	112	45	6	61
Zimbabwe	1	1	0	0

— McNAUGHTON'S HOLY TRINITY —

Irish and Leinster centre Paul McNaughton (1978–1981) played in three of Ireland's sporting shrines in the same year back in 1974. McNaughton, a talented soccer and Gaelic Football player alongside his rugby talents, played for Shelbourne in an FAI Cup final at Dalymount Park, for Wicklow against Louth at Croke Park in the Leinster Senior Football Championship and at Lansdowne Road for Leinster in the same year.

— ROBBIE'S RALEIGH —

Former Lions and Irish scrum-half John Robbie (1976–1981) is now a leading voice on South African radio but the Greystones clubman has an even more unusual claim to fame from his youth.

At the age of four, a cheeky-looking blonde kid called John Robbie appeared in a Christmas TV advertisement for Raleigh bikes. Robbie had to race down the stairs of his house, run towards the Christmas tree, pick up his bike and then proclaim gleefully, "It's a Raleigh".

The advert, which was repeated over a number of Christmases, finished with Robbie cycling his new bike around a tree.

— THE LONG WAIT —

In both 1935 and 1974, Ireland were forced to wait a while to see whether they won the Championship.

In 1935, after losing to England in their first game, Ireland defeated Wales and Scotland but they had to wait for the result of the England and Scotland game a week later to see if they won the Championship. Thankfully, the Scots won 10–7 and the title was Ireland's for only the second time.

It was a similar scenario 39 years later. Ireland completed their campaign – defeat to France, a draw with Wales and wins over England and Scotland – with five points from four matches, which left them one point ahead of both Wales and France, who had to travel to London and Edinburgh respectively in their final fixtures. As had been expected, England beat Wales at Twickenham but surprisingly, Scotland defeated France 19–6 and Ireland won their first title in 23 years.

— IRELAND'S TRIPLE CROWNS: NO. 5, 1982 —

Having been whitewashed in 1981, Ireland weren't expected to do much the following season but as history has proved, that's when they can be at their most dangerous. Victories over England at Twickenham – thanks to Ginger McLoughlin's legendary try – and Wales at Lansdowne Road, set up a Triple Crown-winning game against Scotland in Dublin.

In the end, the game turned out to be all about Ollie Campbell. The out-half was in scintillating form on the afternoon in question, knocking over six penalties and a perfectly executed drop goal to kill off the plucky visitors in front of 50,000 supporters eager to see Ireland's first Triple Crown success in 33 years. Four weeks later Tom Kiernan's side headed to Paris to attempt to win the Grand Slam itself but the lack of game time in between the fixtures hindered Ireland's efforts and they went down to a familiar 22–9 tonking. Despite that defeat at Parc des Princes, Ireland still won the Championship.

Date	Result	Venue
23 Jan 1982	Ireland 20–12 Wales	Lansdowne Road
6 Feb 1982	Ireland 16–15 England	Twickenham
20 Feb 1982	Ireland 21–12 Scotland	Lansdowne Road
20 March 1982	Ireland 9–22 France	Parc des Princes

— NOISY GOES QUIETLY —

The career of Noel 'Noisy' Murphy (1958–69) finished off on a sour note against Wales in Cardiff in 1969. The flanker from the Cork Constitution club was in the middle of his 41st cap for his country at the Arms Park when an unidentified Welsh forward knocked him to floor with a punch off the ball. The Welsh player was warned and penalised by the referee but as Murphy was helped from the field for the final occasion in an Irish shirt, the punishment seemed on the lenient side.

— IRELAND'S LIONS —

The Lions, or the British Isles as they were called back in the late 19th century, first toured Australia and New Zealand in 1888 but it wasn't until their second tour, eight years later, that Ireland got their first representation in the party. There was a decent gang of them, too, with nine players in total chosen to tour South Africa in the summer of 1896, including three players who hadn't previously been capped for their country.

The Irish star in the party was Tom Crean, a doctor and giant of a man who played in all four Tests against South Africa. Crean surprised many by staying on in the country after the tour, first setting up a medical practice in Johannesburg, and then fighting as a medic in the Boer War. But before Crean put his life on the line in battle, he helped the touring side to a three Test to one victory over South Africa. Below is a list of all Irish players to make at least one appearance in a Test game while on tour with the Lions from 1910 to 2005, the tours that had full Test status:

Player	Club	Tour(s)
Bob Alexander	NIFC	1938
George Beamish	Leicester	1930
Vesey Boyle	Dublin University	1938
Norman Brand	NIFC	1924
Barry Bresnihan	UCD	1968
Niall Brophy	UCD	1968
Shane Byrne	Blackrock College	2005
Ollie Campbell	Old Belvedere	1980, 1983
Tom Clifford	Young Munster	1950
George Cromey	Queen's University	1938
William Cunningham	Lansdowne	1924
Jeremy Davidson	London Irish	1997
Ronnie Dawson	Wanderers	1959
Mick Doyle	Blackrock College	1968
Willie Duggan	Blackrock College	1977
Simon Easterby	Llanelli	2005
Jimmy Farrell	Bective Rangers	1930

Ciaran Fitzgerald	St Mary's College	1983
Alexander Foster	Queen's University	1910
Mike Gibson	Cambridge/NIFC	1966, 1968, 1971, 1974, 1977
Bob Graves	Wanderers	1938
Noel Henderson	Queen's University	1950
Rob Henderson	Wasps	2001
Dave Hewitt	Queen's/NIFC	1959, 1962
Denis Hickie	St Mary's College	2005
David Irwin	Instonians	1983
Moss Keane	Lansdowne	1977
Ken Kennedy	London Irish	1966
Michael Kiernan	Dolphin	1983
Tom Kiernan	Cork Constitution	1962, 1968
Jackie Kyle	Queen's University	1950
Ronnie Lamont	Instonians	1966
Mick Lane	UCC	1950
Sean Lynch	St Mary's College	1971
Willie John McBride	Ballymena	1962, 1966, 1968, 1971, 1974
Bill McKay	Queen's University	1950
Harry McKibbin	Queen's University	1938
Ray McLoughlin	Blackrock College	1966
Hugo MacNeill	Oxford	1983
Jim McVicker	Collegians	1924
Blair Mayne	Queen's University	1938
Syd Millar	Ballymena	1959, 1962, 1968
Eric Millar	Leicester	1997
Dick Milliken	Bangor	1974
George Morgan	Clontarf	1938
Bill Mulcahy	UCD	1959, 1962
Karl Mullen	Old Belvedere	1950
Brendan Mullin	London Irish	1989
Andy Mulligan	London Irish	1959
Geordan Murphy	Leicester	2005
Noel Murphy	Cork Constitution	1959, 1966
Paul Murray	Wanderers	1930

Jimmy Nelson	Malone	1950
Donncha O'Callaghan	Cork Constitution	2005
Paul O'Connell	Young Munster	2005
Rodney O'Donnell	St Mary's College	1980
Brian O'Driscoll	Blackrock College	2001, 2005
John O'Driscoll	London Irish	1980, 1983
Ronan O'Gara	Cork Constitution	2005
Henry O'Neill	Queen's University	1930
Tony O'Reilly	Old Belvedere	1955, 1959
Phil Orr	Old Wesley	1977
Colin Patterson	Instonians	1980
Cecil Pedlow	CIYMS	1955
Oliver Piper	Cork Constitution	1910
Nick Popplewell	Greystones	1993
Tom Reid	Garryowen	1955
Trevor Ringland	Ballymena	1983
John Robbie	Greystones	1980
Fergus Slattery	Blackrock College	1974
Tom Smyth	Malone	1910
Colm Tucker	Shannon	1980
Sam Walker	Instonians	1938
Paul Wallace	Saracens	1997
Tony Ward	Garryowen	1980
Gordon Wood	Garryowen	1959
Keith Wood	Harlequins	1997, 2001
Roger Young	Queen's University	1966, 1968

— IRELAND'S MOST MEMORABLE TRIES: SIMON GEOGHEGAN V ENGLAND, 1994 —

It was the moment a much maligned back-line proved their worth. From a line-out drive midway inside the English half, Michael Bradley passed to Eric Elwood, who in turn skipped to Phil Danaher at outside centre. The Garryowen man fixed his man before releasing to the onrushing Richard Wallace on his inside. Wallace then released Geoghegan on the left wing and the winger dived over for a brilliant score.

— THIS IS YOUR LIFE —

Willie John McBride received quite a shock when he walked off the field following the conclusion of the IRFU centenary match between an Ireland and Scotland combination and one from England and Wales at Lansdowne Road on 19 April 1975. Just as he was about to enter the tunnel, McBride was greeted by Eamon Andrews and that evening was the subject of TV's *This is Your Life*.

— SPORTING ALL ROUNDERS —

Irish internationals who have excelled at other sports:

- Mick Galwey (1991–2002) won an All-Ireland Football winner's medal with Kerry in 1986.
- Tony Ward (1978–1987) won an FAI Cup winner's medal with Limerick United in 1982.
- Paul McNaughton (1978–1981) played inter-county football with Wicklow and League of Ireland soccer with Shelbourne.
- Moss Keane (1974–1984) played U21 football for Kerry and won a Sigerson Cup with UCC.
- Gavin Duffy (2004-present) played on the Mayo minor team that lost to Down in the All-Ireland final of 1999 at Croke Park.
- Victor Costello (1996–2004) represented Ireland in the shot put event at the 1992 Barcelona Olympics.

— GIBSON DOES ENGLISH TIME —

Irish centre Mike Gibson shares the record with French legend Philippe Sella for facing England in the most number of internationals. Gibson and the French centre both played against England on 15 separate occasions during their respective careers, with both players playing every minute of every game they started. In total Gibson and Sella each played against England for 1,200 minutes, a total of 20 hours.

— IRISH LEGENDS: CIARAN FITZGERALD —

Fiercely proud: Ciaran Fitzgerald

There's one moment of Ciaran Fitzgerald's career that will forever be remembered. With Ireland level 10–10 with England and needing a victory to clinch the Triple Crown at Lansdowne Road in March 1985, the Irish captain gathered his troops around him during a break in play. "Where's your f**king pride?" were the hooker's immortal words in the huddle and they had the desired effect. Minutes later Michael Kiernan landed a drop goal between the sticks to win the game for Ireland and more than any other memory of the day, Fitzgerald's words have stood the test of time.

If that was the best moment of his career, then there's no doubting the worst. To the annoyance of the British media, Fitzgerald was named as Lions captain for the 1983 tour to Australia and from the day it was confirmed that an Irishman would lead the party, the hooker hardly got a minute's peace. In such a situation, the one thing Fitzgerald needed from his side was a good start to their 18-match tour but the Lions were defeated in their second game against Auckland and the campaign against him began in earnest. One particularly nasty tirade was instigated by English journalist John Reason. In an a piece of astonishing arrogance, Reason argued that Fitzgerald should have been sent off in the first Test for contravening Law 26 of the game. That particular rule states that any player repeatedly infringing any law of the game should be sent from the field of play. Fitzgerald's crime? Constantly throwing the ball crooked into the line-out. That was just a taste of the inane criticism that Fitzgerald had to put up with over the course of the tour but he did develop a sense of humour about it at the time, asking his brother at home during one phone call to "send out another flak jacket because the one I have now is riddled with bullets".

Unsurprisingly, given the commotion in and about the squad, the Lions were whitewashed 4–0 by All Blacks and it was felt in some quarters that Fitzgerald would never recover from the slating he took in New Zealand. But the army officer from Galway wasn't the type of player or person to skulk off into the shadows. Since making his Irish debut on the tour to Australia in 1979, Fitzgerald had never been the type of player to shirk a battle and less than two years after his Lions experience, Fitzgerald captained Ireland to arguably their most spectacular Triple Crown which culminated in that last-gasp victory over England.

The Five Nations of 1986 – where Ireland lost all four of their fixtures – was his last in an Irish shirt but in 1990, after a number of years concentrating on his army commitments, Fitzgerald was appointed Irish coach, succeeding the broad-minded if unsuccessful Jimmy Davidson. While Fitzgerald may have seemed destined to coach Ireland, his stint in charge was pretty miserable, Ireland losing 14 of the 18 games played during his two and a bit years in charge. The 'oh so nearly' moment of his reign came in a 19–18 World Cup quarter-final defeat to Australia in 1991, a game that Ireland led until Michael Lynagh's try in the very last minute.

After resigning from the Ireland job, Fitzgerald took some more time out from the game but his passion for the sport remains undimmed and, in the late 1990s, he returned to coach a succession of Ireland U21 sides. Since then, Fitzgerald has become a regular contributor on rugby matters on RTE radio and television.

Ciaran Fitzgerald
Born: 4 June 1952, Galway
Club: St Mary's College
Caps: 25
Scoring: 5 points (1 try)
Ireland debut: 3 June 1979 v Australia (Brisbane)

— IRELAND'S MOST MEMORABLE TRIES: GORDON HAMILTON V AUSTRALIA, 1991 —

It was the try that nearly earned Ireland a place in the World Cup semi-final. Jim Staples started the moved by gathering the ball in his own half and chipping into space near the left-hand touchline. Jack Clarke then collected his full-back's chip and passed to Gordon Hamilton, who was in support on the winger's inside. Hamilton managed to trundle to the line from 20 yards out and half the Havelock Square End of the old ground came to greet him in the in-goal area. The great pity was that Ireland couldn't hold onto their lead and earn a shot at the World Cup final.

— IRELAND AT THE THIRD RUGBY WORLD CUP: 1995 —

Results and scorers

Pool C

27 May	**Ireland**	**19–43 New Zealand**	Ellis Park
	T: Corkey, Halpin McBride C: Elwood (2)		
31 May	**Ireland**	**50–28 Japan**	Bloemfontein
	T: Corkery, Francis Geoghegan, Halvey Hogan, pen try (2) P: Burke C: Burke (6)		
4 June	**Ireland**	**24–23 Wales**	Ellis Park
	T: Halvey, McBride Popplewell P: Elwood C: Elwood (3)		

RWC Pool C Table

	P	W	D	L	F	A	PTS
New Zealand	3	3	0	0	225	45	9
Ireland	**3**	**2**	**0**	**1**	**93**	**94**	**7**
Wales	3	1	0	2	89	68	5
Japan	3	0	0	3	55	252	3

Quarter-final

10 June	**Ireland**	**12–36 France**	Durban
	P: Elwood (4)		

Squad and Coach

Coach: Gerry Murphy and Noel Murphy

Captain: Terry Kingston

Forwards: D. Corkery (NZ, J, W, F), A. Foley (J (r)), N. Francis (NZ, J, W, F), G. Fulcher (NZ, W, F), G. Halpin (NZ, W, F), E. Halvey (J, W (r), F (r)), P. Johns (NZ, J, W, F) T. Kingston (NZ, J (r), W, F), D. McBride (NZ, W, F), N. Popplewell (NZ, J, W, F), D. Tweed (J), P. Wallace (J), K. Wood (J)

Backs: J. Bell (NZ, W, F), M. Bradley (NZ), P. Burke (J), E. Elwood (NZ, W, F), M. Field (NZ (r), J), S. Geoghegan (NZ, J, W, F), B. Mullin (NZ, J, W, F), C. O'Shea (J, W, F), J. Staples (NZ), R. Wallace (NZ, J, W, F),

Appearances as a replacement marked with (r)

— FOOT-AND-MOUTH —

Four Irish internationals have been cancelled or postponed due to foot-and-mouth disease down the years.

The first came in December 1967, when the touring All Blacks were forced to cancel their game against Ireland at Lansdowne Road. While that particular game was never rescheduled, the rest of Ireland's games postponed because of the disease were later squeezed into the calendar.

After beating Italy and France in February of 2001, the outbreak of foot-and-mouth in Britain forced Ireland's remaining three games against Scotland, Wales and England to be played the following autumn. The rearranged fixtures started badly for Ireland with a defeat away to Scotland, but a victory against Wales in Cardiff and a memorable 20–14 victory over England at Lansdowne Road to deny Clive Woodward's side the Grand Slam, finished the over-extended season off quite nicely for Warren Gatland's men.

— LONGEST LOSING SEQUENCE —

Ireland's longest losing sequence spanned 11 matches between October 1991 and February 1993. The miserable run all started with defeat to Scotland in the 1991 World Cup in Edinburgh and it finally finished with a 19–14 win over Wales in Cardiff on 6 March 1993. Below is a full list of the results:

Date	Result	Venue
12 Oct 1991	Ireland 15–24 Scotland	Murrayfield
20 Oct 1991	Ireland 18–19 Australia	Lansdowne Road
18 Jan 1992	Ireland 15–16 Wales	Lansdowne Road
1 Feb 1992	Ireland 9–38 England	Twickenham
15 Feb 1992	Ireland 10–18 Scotland	Lansdowne Road
21 March 1992	Ireland 12–44 France	Parc des Princes
30 May 1992	Ireland 21–24 New Zealand	Dunedin
6 June 1992	Ireland 6–59 New Zealand	Wellington
31 Oct 1992	Ireland 17–42 Australia	Lansdowne Road
16 Jan 1993	Ireland 3–15 Scotland	Murrayfield
20 Feb 1993	Ireland 6–21 France	Lansdowne Road

— A SHORT HEAD —

Ireland's single point victories:

Date	Result	Venue
26 Feb 1921	Ireland 9–8 Scotland	Lansdowne Road
9 Feb 1929	Ireland 6–5 England	Twickenham
8 Feb 1930	Ireland 4–3 England	Lansdowne Road
14 Feb 1931	Ireland 6–5 England	Twickenham
14 Feb 1948	Ireland 11–10 England	Twickenham
24 Feb 1951	Ireland 6–5 Scotland	Murrayfield
6 March 1976	Ireland 13–12 England	Twickenham
6 Feb 1982	Ireland 16–15 England	Twickenham
19 Feb 1994	Ireland 13–12 England	Twickenham
22 March 2003	Ireland 25–24 Wales	Millennium Stadium
26 Oct 2003	Ireland 16–15 Argentina	Adelaide Oval
10 March 2007	Ireland 19–18 Scotland	Murrayfield

— PROGRAMME PRICES —

A selection of the cost of an Ireland match programmes over time:

Year	Cost
1934	3p
1947	3p
1955	1 shilling
1967	1 shilling
1973	10p
1976	15p
1979	20p
1981	40p
1992	£1.50
1996	£2.00
1999	£2.50
2003	€4.00
2006	€5.00
2007	€5.00

— CON JOB —

Ronan O'Gara and Eric Elwood (1993–1999) jointly hold the Irish record for the number of successful conversions in a single game. Elwood notched ten converts in Ireland's 70–0 victory over Georgia at Lansdowne Road on 14 November 1998, while O'Gara equalled that feat on 11 November 2000 against Japan at Lansdowne Road. In terms of career conversions, O'Gara leads the ways, as listed below:

Cons	Player	Caps	Career
117	Ronan O'Gara	73	2000–
88	David Humphreys	72	1996–2005
43	Eric Elwood	35	1993–1999
40	Michael Kiernan	43	1982–1991
26	Tom Kiernan	54	1960–1973
16	Richard Lloyd	19	1910–1920
15	Ollie Campbell	22	1976–1984

— FIRST WHISTLERS —

Irish referee Mr Abram Combe took charge of Ireland's first ever international against England in 1875. The concept of neutral referees didn't kick-in until 1882, when another Irish referee, Mr H. L. Robinson, took charge of England's game against Scotland in Manchester on 4 March of that year.

— MOST TESTS AS CAPTAIN —

Tests	Player	Span
38	Brian O'Driscoll	2002–
36	Keith Wood	1996–2003
24	Tom Kiernan	1963–1973
19	Ciaran Fitzgerald	1982–1986
17	Fergus Slattery	1979–1981
17	Donal Lenihan	1986–1990

— TROUBLE IN RIO —

On the way home from their summer tour to Argentina in 1970, the entire Irish party were asked to leave their plane in Rio de Janeiro, enroute to Dublin. It was suggested by the airline that some Irish players had been misbehaving on the flight but following a thorough IRFU investigation, this was refuted and the report concluded that the Irish party had been thrown off the plane because of an airline overbooking problem.

Whatever the reason for their stopover, the Irish team had to wait a number of days before they could head for home once more and that wasn't their only problem on the tour. During their tour games in Argentina, the visitors suffered a number of injuries because of the overly physical nature of the opposition. Bill Brown broke a leg, Ronnie Lamont had to spend four days in hospital with concussion while Tom Grace, Syd Millar, Barry McGann and Paddy Madigan all spent time on the sideline with one injury or another.

— IRISH LEGENDS: WILLIE JOHN MCBRIDE —

Willie John!

Very few rugby players the world over can be identified without their surname but that's not the case with 'Willie John'. The Irish and Lions second-row is known the world over by his first name and why wouldn't he be? Over the course of his 13-year international career, McBride earned 63 caps for Ireland and travelled on five different Lions tours, making 17 Test appearances in that famous red shirt.

The odd thing about McBride was that he didn't come from a traditional Irish rugby background. His father died when he was just four and he was brought up by his mother on a small farm in Toomebridge, County Antrim. He was educated at Ballymena Academy and that was where he first came across rugby.

As a teenager, McBride was quite big for his size and he took to the game quite easily, progressing through the ranks at speed until he was selected to make his Irish debut as a 21-year-old against England at Twickenham. Although Ireland lost 16–0 that day, the debutant managed to make quite a decent impression and from that game, until his retirement at the end of the 1975 season, the only internationals McBride missed out on were those when injury ruled out his participation.

While his days in an Irish shirt didn't yield much success, bar one Championship success in 1974, his Lions career was truly special. He travelled on his first tour to South Africa 1962, his debut season as an international, and he packed his bags for a further four trips before his retirement, to New Zealand in 1966 and 1971 and to South Africa again in 1968 and 1974. But it was for that final tour, which McBride captained, that the Ballymena man will be best remembered for.

Heading down to South Africa that year, the Lions weren't given much hope of winning the four-match Test series but McBride had different plans. On his previous two tours against the Springboks, he realised that the home side liked to rely on physical dominance – some legal, most of it not – to win games and McBride decided his side would get their retaliation in before South Africa even knew what was happening to them. The Ulster man thus invented the '99' call (it was to be called '999' but the players felt it was too long), the signal which would instruct every Lion on the pitch to 'take on' their nearest opponent no matter what the situation.

The tactic got its first usage in the provincial game against Eastern Province and once half the home side had been levelled to the ground, word spread around South Africa of the physicality of the Lions. It seemed to work. Over the course of the tour, the Lions won all of their 18 provincial games and also won the Test series 3–0. It would have been 4–0 had a perfectly legitimate Fergus Slattery try not been disallowed in the drawn fourth Test but the Lions left South Africa that summer as the most successful touring side the world had ever known. That they achieved all this under McBride's captaincy was no coincidence whatsoever.

On his return from that final Lions tour, McBride played just one more season but he capped it off with style. In the last minute of his last ever game at Lansdowne Road, against France, the second-row crossed for his first and last Irish try to the sheer delight of the throngs at the Dublin venue. From there, he disappeared from rugby for a couple of years, concentrating for once on his job in the bank in Ballymena, before re-emerging as Ulster coach in the early 1980s. After acting as manager on the unsuccessful 1983 Lions tour to New Zealand, McBride was appointed Irish coach for the 1983/84 season but that period was not another glorious chapter in the career of the Ballymena man. Ireland lost all of their four Championship matches that year and McBride was replaced by Mick Doyle the following season.

Since then, Willie John has worked the after-dinner speech circuit to much acclaim and he still lives in his native Ulster, not far from the farm where he was brought up.

Willie John McBride
Born: 6 June 1940, Antrim
Club: Ballymena
Caps: 63
Scoring: 5 points (1 try)
Ireland debut: 10 February 1962 v England (Twickenham)

— NEUTRAL LANSDOWNE —

Lansdowne Road has hosted four full internationals that have not involved Ireland:

Date	Result	Tournament
27 Oct 1991	Australia 16–6 All Blacks	Rugby World Cup
18 Nov 1998	Romania 27–23 Georgia	RWC Qualifier
9 Oct 1999	USA 25–27 Romania	Rugby World Cup
24 Oct 1999	France 47–26 Argentina	Rugby World Cup

— ONE-CAP HERO —

Derek McAleese holds the unique record of scoring every single one of Ireland's points during his international career. McAleese knocked over four penalties on his debut in Ireland's 44–12 defeat to France on 21 March 1992 at the Parc des Princes. Despite his point-scoring debut, McAleese was never capped for Ireland again.

— IRELAND ON TOUR —

Tours undertaken by Ireland:

Country	Years
Argentina	1952*, 1970*, 2000, 2007
Australia	1967, 1979, 1994, 1999, 2003, 2006
Canada	1889*, 1989*, 2000
Chile	1952*
Fiji	1976*
France	1988*
Japan	1985*, 2005
Namibia	1991
New Zealand	1976, 1992, 2002, 2006
Rhodesia	1961*
South Africa	1961, 1981, 1998, 2004
United States	1989*, 1996, 2000

* *denotes tours where international caps weren't awarded*

— TROPHIES —

Over the past two decades, a multitude of new trophies have appeared to mark individual games between two nations. Below is a list, along with a brief history, of all the trophies that Ireland now compete for on the international stage:

Lansdowne Cup: Established in 1999, the Lansdowne Cup was presented to the Australian Rugby Union by the Lansdowne Club of Sydney and it was competed for between Ireland and the Wallabies. It was designed and manufactured by Waterford Crystal.

Millennium Trophy: This trophy, up for grabs between England and Ireland, was initiated in 1988 to commemorate Dublin's millennium as a city. The trophy is in the shape of a Viking helmet and was donated by computer company Digital.

Six Nations: The Six Nations trophy (or Five Nations trophy as it was previously known) was only established in 1993, despite the competition going on for a good century before that. The trophy is made of 200 ounces of sterling silver and the inside is coated with 22 carat gold to protect it against alcohol erosion. The trophy has 15 sides, representing each player on a rugby team, and the handle on the lid is interchangeable depending on who wins it. The capacity of the trophy is exactly five bottles of champagne, representing the original Five Nations.

Triple Crown: The Triple Crown was the greatest intangible honour in world sport until a trophy was manufactured as reward for winning it in 2006. The trophy is a silver dish measuring 42cm wide and 5cm deep. Ireland were the first team to be awarded the trophy when they beat England at Twickenham in March 2006.

Webb Ellis Cup: The Webb Ellis Cup is awarded to the winner of the Rugby World Cup but it wasn't specifically designed for the tournament. The trophy was created by Garrard's Jewellers of London's Regent Street as far back as 1906 and was brought out of the company's vaults to show IRB committee members in February 1987. Obviously they liked what they saw and they purchased the trophy before christening it the 'William Webb Ellis Cup', after the game's founder. The cup is 38cm in height and is crafted from gilded silver and is supported by two scroll handles.

— IRELAND'S MOST MEMORABLE TRIES: BASIL MACLEAR V SOUTH AFRICA, 1906 —

There were no television cameras around the witness this try but it has gone down in numerous books and journals as a very special solo effort. Basil Maclear gathered the ball inside his own '25' at Ravenhill with a line of South African defenders in front of him. He jinked to evade two desperate South African tackles and then headed off into open country. With a couple of defenders trailing in his jet stream, Maclear finally touched down to the left of the posts to finish off a spectacular try.

— THE MCCAHILL BROTHERS —

Bernie and Sean McCahill both played international rugby as centres in the 1990s but for different countries. Sean earned his one and only cap for Ireland as a sub against Fiji on 18 November 1995, while Bernie made his mark with New Zealand a little earlier than his younger brother. McCahill the elder earned ten All Black caps between 1987 and 1991, scoring one try during his international career.

— MOST CONCEDED —

The international games in which Ireland have conceded the most points:

Conceded	Date	Opposition	Venue
63	15 Nov 1997	New Zealand	Lansdowne Road
59	6 June 1992	New Zealand	Wellington
50	5 Feb 2000	England	Twickenham
46	15 Feb 1997	England	Lansdowne Road
46	12 June 1999	Australia	Brisbane
45	17 Feb 1996	France	Parc des Princes
45	16 Feb 2002	England	Twickenham
45	7 June 2003	Australia	Perth
44	21 March 1992	France	Parc des Princes
44	6 April 2002	France	Stade de France
43	27 May 1995	New Zealand	Ellis Park
43	9 Nov 2003	France	Melbourne
43	11 Feb 2006	France	Stade de France
42	31 Oct 1992	Australia	Lansdowne Road
42	30 March 2003	England	Lansdowne Road

— SMITH SWITCH —

Brian Smith became the first player to be capped for Ireland having previously played for another country. Smith, an out-half by trade, made his Irish debut against New Zealand on 18 November 1989 and went on to win a total of nine Irish caps. Before his career with Ireland, Smith won seven caps with the Wallabies and actually scored a try against Ireland in the 1987 World Cup quarter-final.

— IRELAND'S COACHES —

Ireland's coaches, from Ronnie Dawson to Eddie O'Sullivan:

Coach	Career
Ronnie Dawson	1970–1972
Syd Millar	1972–1975
Roly Meates	1975–1977
Noel Murphy	1977–1980
Tom Kiernan	1980–1983
Willie John McBride	1983–1984
Mick Doyle	1984–1987
Jim Davidson	1987–1990
Ciaran Fitzgerald	1990–1992
Noel Murphy and Gerry Murphy	1992–1995
Murray Kidd	1995–1997
Brian Ashton	1997–1998
Warren Gatland	1998–2001
Eddie O'Sullivan	2001–

— LANSDOWNE WINNERS —

From the period when Italy joined the Six Nations in 2000 until Lansdowne Road closed at the end of the 2006 Championship, Ireland won 15 of their 18 Six Nations games at Lansdowne Road. The three defeats came against Wales in April 2000, England in March 2003 and France in 2005. Three players, Peter Stringer, Brian O'Driscoll and John Hayes, played in all 15 Six Nations victories at Lansdowne.

— IRISH LEGENDS: TONY O'REILLY —

Tony O'Reilly: good at rugby, even better at business

Very few Irish rugby players have made a bigger name for themselves after hanging up their boots but Tony O'Reilly is the big exception. O'Reilly earned 29 Irish caps and travelled on two Lions tours during his career on the pitch but his prowess in the world of business since, and even during, his rugby days have brought the former winger just as much, and arguably even more, recognition and renown.

O'Reilly was educated at Belvedere College on Dublin's North side and it was at school where his rugby career began. Coached and guided by the great Irish captain Karl Mullen, he of Grand Slam winning fame, O'Reilly went straight from school into the Irish team to play France in 1955 aged just 18. Such was his impact on the Five Nations Championship of that year, O'Reilly was selected to tour with the Lions to South Africa that very summer and he proved a revelation. He became the youngest ever Test Lion when he started as a 19-year-old against the Springboks in August of that year in front of a world record crowd of 95,000 at Ellis Park, and he also managed to score a try in a 23–22 win for the tourists. He played in all four Tests in a series that was drawn 2–2 and by the time the tour came to a close, O'Reilly had managed a try tally of 16 in South Africa.

In 1959, he continued his remarkable Lions scoring record on the tour to Australia and New Zealand. O'Reilly played in all six Tests (two against Australia, four against New Zealand) and he managed to cross the line 22 times in all on tour. His tally of 38 tries over two tours is an all-time Lions record that is unlikely to be beaten, as his is tally in Test games of six. Put simply, O'Reilly is the most prolific Lions scorer of all time and the great pity is that he never really played in an Irish team good enough to fully utilise his talents. In 1963, after 28 caps and aged just 27, it appeared that his career in a green shirt was over but there was one more surprise to come.

In 1970, O'Reilly, then the MD of Heinz UK, was selected to play for Ireland against England at Twickenham at the ripe old age of 33. The Thursday before the match, O'Reilly arrived at Irish training in a chauffeur-driven Rolls Royce and the story appeared in all the papers the next day. By the time the game kicked off, England knew that they would be targeting Ireland's comeback kid and early on they launched a garryowen in his general direction. O'Reilly caught the ball and was flattened by half the English pack, who all wanted a piece of him. After the winger eventually got back to his feet, a hush descended on Twickenham, one which was only broken by an Irish voice in the crowd saying, "And you can kick his f**king chauffeur too". Even O'Reilly had to laugh at that one.

Before that surprising comeback, the Dubliner had already made a name for himself in the world of Irish business. His first major job was as general manager of An Bord Bainne (Irish Milk Board) and by 1966 he was managing director of the Irish Sugar Company. He became MD of Heinz UK a year before his surprise recall at Twickenham and from there on it was onwards and upwards. After becoming the first non-Heinz family member to become chairman of the company in 1987, O'Reilly transformed the company into a major global player but he had other business interests besides.

In 1973, he formed Independent News and Media, a group that now owns newspapers in South Africa, Australia as well as the *Independent* titles in both Dublin and London. The company now has over 200 national and regional titles in its stable. O'Reilly also has a host of other business interests and he was knighted by the Queen in the New Years Honours lists of 2001 for his contributions to charity. Today, O'Reilly is listed as number 562 in the Forbes Worldwide Rich List.

Tony O'Reilly
Born: 7 May 1936, Dublin
Club: Old Belvedere
Caps: 29
Scoring: 20 points (4 tries)
Ireland debut: 22 January 1955 v France (Lansdowne Road)

— HAT-TRICK HEROES —

Players who have scored three tries in one match for Ireland:

Player	Date	Opponents	Venue
Rob Montgomery	12 March 1887	Wales	Birkenhead
Joseph Quinn	24 March 1913	France	Mardyke
Eugene Davy	22 Feb 1930	Scotland	Murrayfield
Seamus Byrne	28 Feb 1953	Scotland	Murrayfield
Keith Crossan	1 Nov 1986	Romania	Lansdowne Road
Brendan Mullin	3 June 1987	Tonga	Brisbane
Matt Mostyn	28 Aug 1999	Argentina	Lansdowne Road
Brian O'Driscoll	19 March 2000	France	Stade de France
Mike Mullins	10 June 2000	United States	New Hampshire
Denis Hickie	11 Nov 2000	Japan	Lansdowne Road
Rob Henderson	3 Feb 2001	Italy	Stadio Flaminio
Brian O'Driscoll	2 March 2002	Scotland	Lansdowne Road
Kevin Maggs	17 Nov 2002	Fiji	Lansdowne Road

— MOST CAPPED LIONS PLAYERS —

Two Irish internationals are among the most capped test Lions:

Tests	Player	Career
17	**Willie John McBride (Ireland)**	**1962–1974**
13	Dickie Jeeps (England)	1955–1962
12	**Mike Gibson (Ireland)**	**1966–1977**
12	Graham Price (Wales)	1977–1983

— IRELAND'S TRIPLE CROWNS: NO. 6, 1985 —

Under the stewardship of Mick Doyle, Ireland started their campaign with a last-gasp victory over Scotland at Murrayfield courtesy of a Trevor Ringland try, and after a 15–15 draw with France, a comprehensive victory over Wales in Cardiff set the side up for a tilt at their sixth Triple Crown against England in Dublin.

The game will be best remembered for Ciaran Fitzgerald's "Where's your f**king pride?" comment in the dying minutes of the game but before that it was trench warfare at a wet and windy Lansdowne Road. A Rob Andrew penalty put England in front but then Brendan Mullin blocked down a feeble English kick to cross for Ireland's only try of the game. With 79 minutes on the clock, the game tied at 10–10 and another Triple Crown about to slip from Ireland's grasp, Donal Lenihan led a charge up the centre off a line-out, Michael Bradley whipped the ball back to Michael Kiernan in the pocket and the Dolphin man steadied himself to land the crucial drop goal. The win over England was not just good enough to win Ireland the Triple Crown, it also sealed the Championship for Mick Doyle's brave and adventurous side.

Date	Result	Venue
2 Feb 1985	Ireland 18–15 Scotland	Murrayfield
2 March 1985	Ireland 15–15 France	Lansdowne Road
16 March 1985	Ireland 21–9 Wales	Cardiff Arms Park
20 March 1985	Ireland 13–10 England	Lansdowne Road

— IRISH RUGBY BY NUMBERS —

According to the IRB, Irish rugby has:

201 . . . clubs
100,974 . . . players
2,345 . . . referees
19,984 . . . senior male players
1,756 . . . senior female players

— GIANT KILLINGS —

Ireland have suffered a number of giant killings in international rugby, with a couple of them coming during the reign of Murray Kidd.

On 12 November 1996, Samoa, or Western Samoa as they were then, came to Lansdowne Road and turned the form book upside down by thrashing Ireland 40–25 on their home patch. Less than two months later, on 4 January 1997, Italy came to Dublin and managed the same trick, beating Kidd's side 37–29. Needless to say the Kiwi coach was shown the door by the IRFU but his successor, Brian Ashton, was the victim of another giant killing at the hand of the Italians. The Azzurri beat Ireland 37–22 in Bologna in December 1997, three years before they were admitted to the Six Nations.

However, the most shocking Irish defeat of all came during the 1999 World Cup. Ireland had been expected to negotiate their quarter-final play-off against Argentina in Lens with some comfort but it didn't turn out that way on the day in question. The Pumas clearly had a bee in their bonnet and despite an extraordinary effort from Ireland in the game's dying moments, Argentina won 28–24 to cause arguably the biggest ever shock in Rugby World Cup history.

— LEVEL PEGGING —

Ireland have drawn 28 games of international rugby, 18 at home and 10 away. Their first draw came against England (2–2) on 6 February 1882 at Lansdowne Road, with the last against Canada (27–27) on 17 June 2000. Below is the list of countries that Ireland have drawn against in international rugby:

Draws	**Country**
8	England
6	Wales
5	France and Scotland
1	New Zealand, South Africa, Canada, Argentina

— THE TMO ARRIVES —

Video referees or television match officials (TMO) were first permitted to examine the validity of a try in 2001.

The first time the TMO was called into action in an Irish game was on 17 February of that year when English official Brian Campsall ruled that Brian O'Driscoll did legally touch the ball down over the line against France at Lansdowne Road. The ironic thing about Campsall's decision was that most Irish players and supporters after the game were of the view that the TMO actually made the wrong decision in awarding the try, and that O'Driscoll didn't get downward pressure on the ball as he stretched over the French line eight minutes into the second-half.

Still, it didn't stop anybody celebrating a 22–15 win for the home side.

— IRELAND'S CHAMPIONSHIP WINS —

Ireland have won the Four, Five or Six Nations Championships outright on ten separate occasions:

1894
1896
1899
1935
1948
1949
1951
1974
1982
1985

— PASS RECORD —

At half-time in Ireland's 2006 Six Nations match against France at the Stade de France, the visitors trailed Les Bleus 43–3 at the interval and a record defeat looked on the cards. However, by the time the game finished, the scoreboard read 43–31 in favour of France.

Whether the home side fell asleep in the second half or Ireland actually woke up, we'll probably never know but after that strange game was dissected, it emerged that Ireland had set a new record, 153, for the number of passes in one half of rugby. It was some turnaround from the Six Nations of 2005, where Ireland averaged a total of 106 passes over 80 minutes of rugby.

— MOST TRIES IN A SEASON —

Brian O'Driscoll is one of two Irish players to share the honour of having scored the most tries (five) in a championship season.

The exotically named Jack 'Joxer' Arigho achieved the same feat as the current Irish captain back in 1928, a season when Ireland were denied a Triple Crown by a last day defeat to Scotland. O'Driscoll achieved his tally of five tries in the Six Nations Championship of 2000.

— WHITE LINE DROUGHT —

The longest Ireland have ever gone without scoring an international try is seven games, and even that can be forgiven when you consider these were their first seven games of international rugby.

From Ireland's first game against England in 1875 up to and including their fixture against the same opposition in 1879, the new boys couldn't manage a try but the drought was finally broken the following season by John Loftus Cuppaidge's effort against England at Lansdowne Road.

— IRELAND AT THE FOURTH RUGBY WORLD CUP: 1999 —

Results and scorers
Pool E

2 Oct	**Ireland**	**53–8 USA**	Lansdowne Road
	T: Wood (4), Bishop Pen Try, O'Driscoll P: Humphreys (2) C: Elwood (2)		
10 Oct	**Ireland**	**3–23 Australia**	Lansdowne Road
	P: Humphreys		
15 Oct	**Ireland**	**44–14 Romania**	Lansdowne Road
	T: O'Shea (2), Ward O'Cuinneagain, Tierney P: Elwood (2) C: Elwood (5) DG: O'Driscoll		

RWC Pool E Table

	P	W	D	L	F	A	PTS
Australia	3	3	0	0	135	31	6
Ireland	**3**	**2**	**0**	**1**	**100**	**45**	**4**
Romania	3	1	0	2	50	126	2
USA	3	0	0	3	52	135	0

Quarter-final play-off

20 Oct	**Ireland**	**24–28 Argentina**	Lens
	P: Humphreys (7) DG: Humphreys		

Squad and Coach
Coach: Warren Gatland
Captain: Dion O'Cuinneagain

Forwards: T. Brennan (US, A), B. Casey (A (r), Ar (r)), P. Clohessy (US, A (r)), J. Davidson (US, Ar), J. Fitzpatrick (USA (r), A, R, Ar (r)), P. Johns (USA, A), A. McKeen (R (r)), E. Miller (US (r), A (r), Ar (r)), R. Nesdale (USA (r), R), D. O'Cuinneagain (US, A, R, Ar), M. O'Kelly (USA (r), A, R, Ar), A. Quinlan (R (r)), P. Wallace (US, A, R, Ar), A. Ward (US, A, R, Ar), K. Wood (US, A, Ar)

Backs: J. Bell (US (r), A (r), R), J. Bishop (US, A, R, Ar), G. D'Arcy (R (r)), E. Elwood (US (r), A (r), R), D. Humphreys (US, A, Ar), K. Maggs (US, A, Ar), M. Mostyn (US, A, R, Ar), B. O'Driscoll (US, A, Ar), B. O'Meara (US (r), R (r)), C. O'Shea (US, A, R, Ar), T. Tierney (US, A, R, Ar)

Appearances as a replacement marked with (r)

— TANAISTE DROPS THE BALL —

Dick Spring, who earned three Irish caps in 1979 went on to become a Labour TD for Kerry North and he later served as Tanaiste (Deputy Prime Minister) from 1982 to 1987 and again from 1992 to 1994.

Although Spring was involved in a lot of high profile incidents during his political career, the memory that most Irish rugby fans have of him stems from a infamous gaffe during his international rugby career. When playing at full-back for Ireland against Wales at Cardiff Arms Park in 1979, Spring failed to gather a garryowen underneath his own posts, allowing Wales to get in for a simple try.

Spring, whose brother Donal also played for Ireland in the second-row, retained his place for Ireland's next Five Nations game against England but after that season he was never selected in the green jersey again.

— WHAT A CLIMAX —

The climax to the 2007 Six Nations Championship was one of the most fascinating in the history of the tournament.

After Ireland had beaten Italy 51–24 in Rome, France knew that they needed to beat Scotland by 24 points in Paris to win the title. As the Irish side watched proceedings unfold from their Rome hotel, France led by just six points at the interval and Ireland were seemingly on course to win their first championship in 22 years. Then the first Irish official in Paris put his stamp on proceedings. Touch judge Donal Courtney from Dublin erroneously sent Scottish winger Sean Lamont to the sin-bin instead of his brother Rory and, with the visitors down to 14 men, France piled on the tries.

France were in the driving seat now thanks to their 27-point lead but with just three minutes left on the clock, Scottish prop Euan Murray crossed for a try that was converted to bring the gap down to 20 and Ireland were in pole position once more.

Then came the intervention from the second Irish official on duty at the Stade de France. Television Match Official Simon McDowell from Belfast was asked to adjudicate as to whether a French rolling maul in injury time had been grounded legally. Replays suggested that McDowell could genuinely have given the call either way but he awarded the try and France sneaked the title ahead of Eddie O'Sullivan's side – with a little help from their Irish friends.

— LAND OF THE RISING SUN —

Ireland's proposed tour to Argentina in the summer of 1985 had to be called off after the UAR (Argentinean Rugby Union) couldn't guarantee the safety of Mick Doyle's players in the aftermath of the Falklands War. Instead, Ireland accepted an invitation to tour Japan for the first time and, not surprisingly, the Triple Crown winners won all five tour matches, including the two Tests against the national side.

— IRISH LEGENDS: TONY WARD —

The flamboyant Tony Ward

One of Oscar Wilde's many aphorisms could have been applied directly to Tony Ward. "The public is wonderfully tolerant," wrote the great Irish playwright. "It forgives everything except genius." All his rugby career, which should have been a lot more glittering given his natural talent, Ward's abilities were mistrusted not only by the sages on the terraces but more importantly, by those whose task it was to pick the team. Narrow-mindedness was always Ward's greatest opponent.

The period that defined his career came at the end of the 1978/79 season. Having started all of Ireland's internationals in both the 1978 and 1979 Five Nations Championships, and performed well in each and every game, Ward travelled on that summer's tour to Australia as Ireland's first choice number ten, with Ollie Campbell seemingly travelling as his replacement. The out-half did everything that could be asked of him in two warm-up games down under but he was then inexplicably dropped for the first Test against the Wallabies. No reasonable explanation has ever been offered for Ward's exclusion at the expense of Campbell and the only obvious answer surrounds old-fashioned IRFU attitudes at the time.

Ward came into the Irish rugby scene with considerable hype surrounding him. Not only did he possess poster-boy looks, the out-half also played the game in flamboyant fashion, running the ball at every given opportunity, even if his skills with the boot were better than most. In many ways he was Irish rugby's first superstar, a player who garnered more media attention than all his team-mates combined.

The fact that he also played League of Ireland soccer with both Shamrock Rovers, and later, Limerick United, would not have done much to endear him to the IRFU committee types who would have avoided watching the round ball game at all costs.

The most likely explanation for his puzzling treatment by the IRFU, then, is that Ward appeared on the Irish rugby scene before Irish rugby was really ready for him. The fact that Campbell played extremely well in Ireland's ground breaking 2–0 Test victory over the Wallabies in the summer of 1979 also contributed to holding Ward's genius back.

Still, it wasn't as though Ward gave up the ghost after that tour. He earned a further ten caps after that summer of disappointment, most of them, admittedly, when either Campbell or his successor, Paul Dean, were injured. He also travelled on the 1980 Lions tour to South Africa and scored a Lions record 18 points in the first Test against the Springboks. Typically, he owed his selection in that game to an injury to Campbell but, cruelly, a thigh muscle injury then ruled Ward out of the tour.

To speak only about Ward's rugby career, though, would be doing his soccer talent a disservice. Ward played League of Ireland soccer for both Shamrock Rovers and Limerick United, winning an FAI Cup winner's medal with the latter in 1982. Perhaps the greatest compliment to his prowess in the round ball game came after he played for Limerick against Southampton in the 1981 UEFA Cup. "With full-time coaching," Saints boss Laurie McMenemy said after the game at the Dell, "it would not take much to play him in higher company."

Ward earned his last Irish cap against Tonga in the 1987 World Cup and he now earns a crust as a rugby journalist for the *Irish Independent*, as well as appearing on RTE television as a pundit and coaching schools rugby.

Tony Ward
Born: 8 October 1954, Dublin
Club: Garryowen and St Mary's
Caps: 19
Scoring: 113 points (29 pens, 7 cons, 4 dgs)
Ireland debut: 21 January 1978 v Scotland (Lansdowne Road)

— TURNCOATS PLAY AT 'HOME' —

Two Irish-born English internationals have played for their adopted country against the nation of their birth at Lansdowne Road. Kyran Bracken, a World Cup winner with England in Australia, featured in four matches for England against Ireland in Dublin between 1995 and 2003. Wilfred Bolton, who was also born in Ireland, turned out on three occasions for England at Lansdowne Road between 1882 and 1887.

— FACES FOR TELEVISION —

The Irish internationals to appear in TV advertisements:

Player	Product
Denis Hickie	Wavin Piping
Paul O'Connell	Powerade
Brian O'Driscoll	Seafield Golf and Country Club and O2
Ronan O'Gara	Lucozade Sport
Peter Stringer	Lucozade Sport
Keith Wood	Dawn Milk and Nike

— MOST TEST LIONS TRIES —

Tony O'Reilly heads the list of the most tries scored by a Lions player in Tests:

Tries	Player	Matches	Career
6	**Tony O'Reilly (Ireland)**	**10**	**1955–1959**
5	JJ Williams (Wales)	7	1974–1977
4	MJ Price (Wales)	5	1904

— TRIPLE CROWN —

Ireland, more so than any other country, have long been besotted by the Triple Crown and it's little surprise that the first recorded account of the term comes from an article in *The Irish Times* article from 12 March 1884.

"After long years of seemingly hopeless struggle Ireland has achieved the triple crown of rugby honours," the paper's anonymous rugby correspondent wrote. The name may also derive from the Triple Crown of James I who was the first King to rule over England, Scotland and Ireland (Wales was considered part of England back then).

— MOST CAPPED IN POSITION —

The most capped Irish players by position:

Position	Player	Caps	Career
Full-back	Tom Kiernan	54	1960–1973
Wing	Denis Hickie	58	1997–
Centre	Brian O'Driscoll	74	1999–
Out-half	Ronan O'Gara	73	2000–
Scrum-half	Peter Stringer	76	2000–
Prop	John Hayes	73	2000–
Second-row	Malcolm O'Kelly	85	1997–
Flanker	Fergus Slattery	61	1970–1984
Number 8	Anthony Foley	62	1995–2006

— CONNACHT LIVE TO FIGHT ANOTHER DAY —

The IRFU were forced into one of the most embarrassing climb downs in their history back in 2002 when they were forced to abandon their plans to disband Connacht as a professional outfit.

With the Union in some financial difficulty at the start of the new millennium, the theory was floated by the IRFU hierarchy that the best way to extricate themselves from the problem would be to disband Connacht and operate just three professional provinces instead.

But while many in the Union saw the province's axing as a *fait accompli*, Connacht began to mobilise the support of the masses. A newly formed supporters group 'Friends of Connacht' was formed and towards the end of January 2003, 2,000 people from the west made their way to the capital to march on Lansdowne Road.

Sensing that public opinion was swinging against them, the IRFU issued a statement on 30 January to the effect that Irish rugby would proceed with four provinces. People power had won out.

— IRELAND BY GOOGLE —

Number of website pages produced by a google search for the following Irish internationals or coaches:

Paul O'Connell	1.3 million
Peter Stringer	1.14 million
Willie John McBride	897,000
Eddie O'Sullivan	602,000
Gordon D'Arcy	495,000
Jerry Flannery	461,000
Brian O'Driscoll	410,000
Shane Horgan	157,000
Ronan O'Gara	111,000
Denis Hickie	74,500

— MOUSTACHES —

Ireland's moustached XV:

15 Dick Spring
14 Freddie McLennan
13 Phil Rainey
12 Paul McNaughton
11 Dolway Walkington
10 Paul Dean
9 Donal Caniffe

1 Phil Orr
2 Justin Fitzpatrick (a prop out of position!)
3 Des Fitzgerald
4 Willie Anderson
5 Donal Lenihan
6 Nigel Carr
7 Phillip Matthews
8 Donal Spring

— THE ALL-IRELAND LEAGUE —

The All-Ireland League, the premier competition for Ireland's senior clubs, was founded in 1990 with clubs from Munster dominating its list of winners:

Year	Winner
1991	Cork Constitution
1992	Garryowen
1993	Young Munster
1994	Garryowen
1995	Shannon
1996	Shannon
1997	Shannon
1998	Shannon
1999	Cork Constitution
2000	St Mary's College
2001	Dungannon
2002	Shannon
2003	Ballymena
2004	Shannon
2005	Shannon
2006	Shannon
2007	Garryowen

— IRFU CENTENARY CELEBRATIONS —

The IRFU celebrated its centenary in the 1974/75 season with a number of special events.

In September 1974 a President's XV, drawn from seven nations, played Ireland. Full caps were awarded for the fixture, which finished 18–18. Then, New Zealand arrived to play all four provinces, the combined universities and the international side. Typically, there was nothing to celebrate from an Irish point of view with the All Blacks winning all six games on their mini-tour.

The celebrations were finished off on 19 April at Lansdowne Road when an Ireland and Scotland combination beat a selection from England and Wales 17–10.

— IRISH LEGENDS: MIKE GIBSON —

Mike Gibson: dedication and talent to burn

Irish rugby has had plenty of truly dedicated players through the decades, and lots of players too with talent to burn, but looking back on Mike Gibson's career you can't help but think that the centre from Belfast was the perfect amalgamation of both.

What set Gibson apart from other Irish players during his career, indeed players from any country you wish to mention at the time, was his extraordinary dedication to the game in an era where a man also had to hold down a full-time job. Although Gibson possessed an amazing skills set – sleight of hand, speed, an ability to beat a man – he never took them for granted and constantly worked on his game, especially the basics that could have been beneath him. That unerring devotion, combined with his acute tactical appreciation for the game, were the main contributory factors to Gibson playing international rugby for 16 seasons, a quite unbelievable stretch that is hardly likely to be replicated by anyone in the future.

Gibson attended the famed rugby nursery Campbell College in Belfast and he made his Irish debut as a 22-year-old while studying law at Cambridge University. He made an immediate impact, playing an important role in Ireland's first win at Twickenham in 16 years. Like Willie John McBride, Gibson's only real success in an Irish shirt came with the 1974 Championship win and it would have been fascinating to see what Gibson could have achieved in a more prosperous era.

Like McBride, however, Gibson really excelled when on the Lions' stage. The Ulster man travelled on five Lions tours in total – 1966, 1968, 1971, 1974, 1977 – and it would be fair to say he made his mark on every single one of them. But it was on the tour of New Zealand in 1971 that Gibson truly flourished. While the likes of Barry John and J.P.R. Williams might have featured more on the highlights reel, it was the class of Gibson, midway between them on the pitch, that underpinned much of what the other two did, helping the Lions to a famous 2–1 series win. His contribution was recognised by the All Black management, who highlighted Gibson as the one player they'd like to have on their side once the series came to an end.

While he was often moved to the wing in his final days in an Irish shirt, a period when he became the oldest player to play for his country, Gibson's star was still as high as ever. In his final Test for Ireland, a victory over Australia in Sydney, Willie Duggan was forced to do something out of the ordinary to recognise his team-mate's efforts on the day. "I wouldn't be a great one for congratulating people on their performances – I've never done that in my life – but the second Test Mike Gibson played for Ireland in Australia in 1979 was absolutely unbelievable," says Duggan. "You would not believe an individual could do so much. It was the first time I ever crossed the dressing-room to shake someone's hand."

On retirement from rugby, Gibson was able to dedicate himself completely to law and he remains head of litigation at Tughans Solicitors in Belfast.

Mike Gibson
Born: 3 December 1942, Belfast
Club: Cambridge University, NIFC
Caps: 69
Scoring: 125 points (9 tries, 16 pens, 7 cons, 6 dgs)
Ireland debut: 8 February 1964 v England (Twickenham)

— IRELAND'S TRIPLE CROWNS: NO. 7, 2004 —

Ireland's campaign started with a heavy defeat in Paris but a big win over Wales at Lansdowne Road and a brave victory over England at Twickenham set up a Triple Crown game against Scotland. On a memorable day at IRFU headquarters, one week after Ireland had brushed aside the challenge of Italy, Scotland threatened to ruin things with a stubborn display despite a poor showing up to that. But tries from Geordan Murphy, Peter Stringer, David Wallace and a brace from Gordon D'Arcy ensured that Ireland held their nerve on the big occasion.

Date	Result	Venue
14 Feb 2004	Ireland 17–35 France	Stade de France
22 Feb 2004	Ireland 36–15 Wales	Lansdowne Road
6 March 2004	Ireland 19–13 England	Twickenham
20 March 2004	Ireland 19–3 Italy	Lansdowne Road
27 March 2004	Ireland 37–16 Scotland	Lansdowne Road

— NICKNAMES —

Irish internationals with interesting nicknames:

Name	**Nickname**
Shane Horgan	Shaggy
Marcus Horan	Puppy
John Hayes	The Bull
Roger Young	Koo Koo
Shane Byrne	Munch
Peter Clohessy	The Claw
Mick Galwey	Gaillimh
Anthony Foley	Axel
Donal Lenihan	Mannix
Ronan O'Gara	Rog
Jack Arigho	Joxer
Noel Murphy	Noisy

— WOODEN SPOON —

Ireland's Wooden Spoons through the decades:

1880s: 1 (1884)
1890s: 1 (1891)
1900s: 1 (1909)
1920s: 1 (1920)
1930s: 2 (1934, 1938)
1950s: 2 (1955, 1958)
1960s: 4 (1960, 1961, 1962, 1964)
1970s: 1 (1977)
1980s: 3 (1981, 1984, 1986)
1990s: 4 (1992, 1996, 1997, 1998)

— THE HEINEKEN CUP —

Irish teams have played a significant role in the development of the European Cup since its inception at the start of the 1995/96 season. Ulster were the first Irish team to win the competition in 1999, while Munster finally brought the trophy home at the third attempt by beating Biarritz in Cardiff in 2006. Below is a record of the 12 Heineken Cup finals that have been played to date:

Date	Result	Venue
20 May 2007	Wasps 25–9 Leicester	Twickenham
20 May 2006	**Munster 23–19 Biarritz**	**Millennium Stadium**
22 May 2005	Toulouse 18–12 Stade Francais	Murrayfield
23 May 2004	Wasps 27–20 Toulouse	Twickenham
24 May 2003	Toulouse 22–17 Perpignan	Lansdowne Road
25 May 2002	**Leicester 15–9 Munster**	**Millennium Stadium**
19 May 2001	Leicester 34–30 Stade Francais	Parc des Princes
27 May 2000	**Nothampton 9–8 Munster**	**Twickenham**
30 Jan 1999	**Ulster 21–6 Colomiers**	**Lansdowne Road**
31 Jan 1998	Bath 19–18 Brive	Stade Lescure
31 Jan 1997	Brive 28–9 Leicester	Cardiff Arms Park
6 Jan 1996	Toulouse 21–18 Cardiff	Cardiff Arms Park

— ROLL CALL —

The most popular surnames of Irish rugby internationals:

Brown	8 *
Kennedy	8
Murphy	8
O'Connor	8
Moore	7
Wallace	7
Fitzgerald	6
Hewitt	6
Johnston	6
Ross	6

* *Total is 12 if you include those spelt Browne*

— DAVE GALLAHER —

The first ever captain of the All Blacks was an Irishman. Dave Gallaher was born in Ramelton, County Donegal on 30 October 1873 and he travelled with his family on the Lady Jocelyn Steam Ship to New Zealand in the spring of 1878. The family of ten children initially settled on a farm in the Bay of Plenty and in 1893 they shifted base to Auckland, where young David first picked up the oval ball. He had an immediate talent and love for the sport; local reports from the time often mention his almost manic zeal for the physical side of the game. It was to be his trademark.

He progressed through the ranks at Auckland and made his debut for the provincial side as a 23-year-old in 1896, all the time working at the Auckland Freezer Company as a foreman. He enlisted in the New Zealand army in 1899 and went off to fight in the Boer War. In three hard years of battle in Transcall, Orange Free State and Cape Town, Gallaher progressed from private to squadron sergeant. When he came home the New Zealand rugby team was being born as a concept, and there was only one man ever going to lead them in their first international. Gallaher skippered his country against Australia in Sydney, the first of his 36 appearances for the national side. Typically, they won.

But it's the Originals tour that Gallaher will be remembered for. The trip to the northern hemisphere by boat took six weeks, and although he had to survive a coup on the way over after his intense training methods were questioned, New Zealand immediately dazzled with the style in which they went about their game.

Rugby in Britain and Ireland had, up until that point, been played around the fringes of the ruck and maul but the visitors were keen to get their backs involved on a more frequent basis. And that's where Gallaher came into his own. He pioneered a new position in rugby, the 'winging forward' as it was called back then. Previously, all teams had entered eight men into the scrum but Gallaher changed all that by using a 2-3-2 formation, employing himself as scrum-half from set-pieces and thus allowing his backline to have additional numbers. And because the captain was loose of the scrum, he was able to get right in the faces of the opposition before anyone else.

Throughout his playing career he wore his shin guards outside his socks. It made him look some kind of Robo-Cop type figure, almost superhuman in a way. The All Blacks (they picked up the name for the first time during the tour) lost one game on their travels. It came against Wales at the Cardiff Arms Park, the home side winning somewhat controversially 3–0 after the All Blacks had what appeared to have been a perfectly good try disallowed in the second half by the Welsh match official.

When the team eventually arrived back in Auckland in early 1906, they were carried off the boat and through the streets of the harbour city. From there, Gallaher played a few more times for the All Blacks before he turned his hand to coaching with Auckland.

In 1917 he volunteered for service in the New Zealand wing of the Allied Forces. A leader to the last, he was promoted to Sergeant within two months of his arrival but was killed at Passchendale on 4 October, 1917. In 2005, Letterkenny Rugby Club, the club nearest to Gallaher's birthplace, decided to name their grounds 'Dave Gallaher Memorial Park'.

— IRELAND AND THE POPE —

The Irish rugby team were granted a special audience with Pope John Paul II before their Six Nations match against Italy in Rome in February 2001. Twenty-nine players and three members of the management team attended the weekly audience in the Vatican City and were afterwards received individually by the Pope. The one player the audience appeared to rub off on was Rob Henderson, who scored a hat-trick of tries the following Saturday against Italy in Ireland's 41–22 victory.

— LANSDOWNE ROAD REDVELOPMENT —

Lansdowne Road hosted its final rugby game in its old guise on 31 December 2006 when Leinster defeated Ulster in a Magners League game. The new Lansdowne Road is expected to rise from the ashes of the old one and be ready to host international rugby once more in December 2009. Below is a timeline of the old stadium, from the day it hosted its first rugby game, to its projected re-opening in 2009:

1872: Venue rented by Henry Dunlop from Earl of Pembroke. First used as an athletics venue but then Lansdowne RFC started to play rugby there later that year.

1876: First representative match between Leinster and Ulster is played there.

1878: First international between Ireland and England played at the Dublin 4 venue. IRFU rent the ground for £5.

1880: Wanderers erect their clubhouse at the opposite end to Lansdowne's.

1900: First football match is stage between Ireland and England.

1906: Lease is signed over to IRFU from Henry Dunlop after his death.

1907: First uncovered stand built at the venue on the West side.

1926: Irish Free State play Italy in a football international.

1927: The first East Stand is built.

1954: The West Upper Stand is built complete with 8,000 seats.

1971: The FAI sign a lease to play football internationals at Lansdowne.

1974: IRFU buys freehold of Lansdowne Road.

1978: Lower tier of the West Stand refurbished.

1983: East Stand demolished and a new one built.

1995: Floodlights erected at the venue for the first time.

2006: Last match at the venue before redevelopment is played between Leinster and Ulster, the first sides to play a representative fixture there.

2007: Demolition of stadium begins in May after planning permission is granted.

2009: 50,000 all-seater stadium expected to open in December.

— NIGHT OF THE LONG KNIVES —

Ireland's Kiwi coach Warren Gatland was given the boot back in November 2001 just a couple of weeks after he almost led his adopted country to their first ever win over his native land.

At half-time in Ireland's 17 November clash against the All Blacks at Lansdowne Road, the home side led 14–7 and after David Wallace crossed the Kiwi line just after the break, Ireland's lead was an incredible 14 points. Unfortunately for all those waiting to watch a bit of history, the All Blacks came back strong in the final half hour, eventually winning the game 40–29. On 28 November, following a review of the November internationals with the IRFU, Gatland was informed that his contract would not be extended and would instead be terminated immediately. As the Kiwi coach left the hotel where the meeting was taking place, his then assistant Eddie O'Sullivan strolled in to meet the IRFU about replacing Gatland.

— IRELAND'S TRIPLE CROWNS: NO. 8, 2006 —

A 31–5 thrashing of Wales at Lansdowne Road got Ireland's Triple Crown bid in motion, and a tetchy 15–9 victory over Scotland at the same venue set up a crunch game against England at Twickenham. For the vast majority of the game, it looked like Andy Robinson's side would crush Irish dreams of an eighth Triple Crown but there was a dramatic twist in the game's final moments. With Ireland 24–21 behind heading into injury-time, the visitors decided to have a go from a scrum inside their own 22. Ronan O'Gara chipped the ball over the English defence, Brian O'Driscoll caught it and released Shane Horgan down the right-hand touchline. The Irish winger was eventually stopped near the English line but after the ball was recycled a couple of times, Peter Stringer found Horgan on the touchline and he stretched over the line from a couple of yards out to seal another memorable Twickenham victory.

Date	Result	Venue
4 Feb 2006	Ireland 26–16 Italy	Lansdowne Road
11 Feb 2006	Ireland 31–43 France	Stade de France
26 Feb 2006	Ireland 31–5 Wales	Lansdowne Road
11 March 2006	Ireland 15–9 Scotland	Lansdowne Road
18 March 2006	Ireland 28–24 England	Twickenham

— LEWIS'S CRICKET RECORD —

Irish international referee Alan Lewis earned a record 122 caps for the Irish cricket team during his days at the crease. Lewis also captained the Irish side on a number of occasions before his retirement from representative cricket in 1997. The insurance broker took up rugby refereeing in 1989 and refereed his first international in September 1998 when Australia played Fiji at the Parramatta Stadium in Sydney.

— WHELAN'S TOILET TROUBLE —

Irish manager Pat Whelan resigned in controversial circumstances in 1998. The former Munster and Ireland hooker, who earned 19 caps for his country, was Irish manager during Brian Ashton's unsuccessful stint as Irish coach and he continued in the same role when Warren Gatland took over the reigns.

Whelan attracted a lot of media criticism during Ashton's era in charge and when he encountered *Sunday Times* journalist Tom English in the toilet of *The Brazen Head* bar in Limerick late one Sunday night, he took revenge for what the journalist had written about him some months previously.

Whelan attacked English, landing a number of punches, and the incident was widely reported by the media over the coming days. Whelan announced his resignation on the Wednesday and while the official reason given by the IRFU was that their manager was leaving because of "work pressures", there's little doubt that the English toilet incident had something to do with it.

— THE WOMEN'S GAME —

Women's rugby has been played in Ireland since the early 1970s but it wasn't until 1992 that the Irish Women's Rugby Football Union (IWRFU) was formed.

The game was initially played solely among the Irish universities but once the IWRFU came into being, clubs sprouted up all over the country. The first Irish women's international took place against Scotland in February 1993 and since then the side have been a regular competitor in Five and Six Nations competitions, as well as playing in two World Cup Finals. The IWRFU became officially affiliated to the IRFU in February 2001 and there are believed to be 1,800 women playing the game in the country.

— IRISH LEGENDS: TOM KIERNAN —

Greatness can be measured in a number of different ways, none of them definitive, but if overall contribution was the yardstick by which those involved in Irish rugby were graded, Tom Kiernan would undoubtedly be top of the class. As first a player, then a coach and finally an administrator, Cork-born Kiernan has given incredible service to Irish rugby and while the game in this country has had the benefit of countless dedicated people down the years, few have had as much influence, and indeed success, as the Cork Constitution clubman.

As a player, Kiernan was a full-back noted for his on-field intelligence and his 54-cap international career, spanning 13 years was full of glittering achievement. He captained Ireland for what was back then a record 24 times between 1963 and 1973, a period during which he was also de facto coach, such was the way rugby was organised at the time. He also travelled on two Lions tours, the trips to South Africa in 1962 and 1968, captaining the side in that latter unsuccessful tour.

While Ireland and the Lions might not have achieved that much during his days on the pitch, Kiernan was involved with a number of successful Munster teams in the 1960s and 1970s. He was full-back and captain for the province's historic victory over the touring Wallabies in 1967, a position he retained for the 3–3 draw against the All Blacks six years later. Most famously perhaps, after he hung up his boots and turned his hands to coaching, Kiernan coached the legendary Munster team that beat the All Blacks 12–0 on 31 October 1978 in Thomond Park. While his players obviously excelled on the day, Kiernan's coaching and preparation for that game certainly helped. The squad flew to London to play a couple of warm-up games a couple of months before the match, while they trained almost like professionals in the six weeks before the game. His man management of certain players in the build-up to the game was also crucial, with some taking the field like men possessed.

After his historic moment with Munster, Kiernan was appointed Irish coach in 1980, a position he held until the end of the 1983 Five Nations. While he presided over a couple of barren seasons, Ireland did win the Triple Crown in 1982 and in many ways Kiernan was unfortunate not to lead his side to a second Grand Slam. Having clinched the Triple Crown on 20 February against Scotland at Lansdowne Road, Ireland didn't play France until 20 March in Paris. Although his side were beaten 22–9 in their final game, Kiernan always felt that his confident side could have beaten *Les Bleues* had the game been fixed for two weeks earlier.

After he left the Irish job in 1983, Kiernan concentrated his efforts on the administrative side of the game and he had no less influence on matters than he did in the previous two chapters of his rugby life. Kiernan was Ireland's representative on the International Rugby Board (IRB) for a number of years, but he'll probably be best remembered as an administrator for helping to initiate the European Cup.

In the summer of 1995, just after that South African World Cup, the Super 10 competition in the Southern Hemisphere admitted a further two teams to the fold and signed a ten-year, multi-million dollar deal with Sky TV. It was against this background, and while most countries were still in South Africa towards the end of the World Cup, that Welshman Vernon Pugh, with the help of Kiernan, called a meeting of the Five Nations in Johannesburg to discuss the creation of a European equivalent to the Super 12. Their idea was met positively by most unions, the English excepted, and it was agreed that the first European Rugby Cup would be run during the 1995/96 season. The competition has progressed onwards and upwards ever since, all thanks to Kiernan and Pugh's brainwave in South Africa.

In October 2007, Kiernan was inducted into the International Rugby Hall of Fame, a just reward for his enormous contribution to rugby over 50 or so years.

Tom Kiernan
Born: 7 January 1939, Cork
Club: Cork Constitution
Caps: 54
Scoring: 161 (2 tries, 31 pens, 26 cons, 2 dgs)
Ireland debut: 13 February 1960 v England (Twickenham)

— IRELAND'S MOST MEMORABLE TRIES: GERRY MCLOUGHLIN V ENGLAND, 1982 —

It's probably one of the least aesthetically pleasing Irish tries of all time but the context, and McLoughlin's comments afterwards, have ensured that it lingers long in the memory.

After a bit of scrappy play near the right-hand touchline inside the English 22, McLoughlin caught hold of the loose ball, tucked it under his arm and charged at the home side's full-back, Marcus Rose. Rose half-tackled the Irish prop and players from both sides formed to join a rolling maul. The momentum went Ireland's way and a couple of seconds later they crashed over the English line with McLoughlin still holding the ball. When it as suggested to the prop by a BBC reporter that he was helped a little by the pushing of his team-mates from behind, a razor sharp McLoughlin replied: "Pushing? Sure I pulled them all over the line with me."

— OLDEST IRISH DEBUT —

Davy Tweed became the oldest Irish player to make his international debut when he played against France at Lansdowne Road on 4 March 1995. The big second-row from Ballymena was 35-years-old when he won the first of his four Irish caps, the last coming against Japan during the 1995 World Cup in South Africa. Tweed later went on to become a DUP Councillor for Ballymena Council.

— IN THE BIN —

Paddy Johns became the first Irish player to be sent to the sin-bin on 19 March 2000. The second-row from Ulster had only been on the pitch against France for a few minutes as a substitute before he was given a yellow card by referee Paul Honiss for killing the ball on the ground. Although Ireland went on to win the game 27–25, Johns was dropped from the squad for Warren Gatland side's final Six Nations fixture against Wales at Lansdowne Road.

— IRELAND AT THE FIFTH RUGBY WORLD CUP: 2003 —

Results and scorers
Pool A

11 Oct	**Ireland 45–11 Romania**	Gosford
	T: Hickie (2), Horgan Wood, Costello P: Humphreys (4) C: Humphreys (3), O'Gara	
19 Oct	**Ireland 64–7 Namibia**	Sydney
	T: Miller (2), Quinlan (2) Dempsey, Horgan, Hickie, Horan, Easterby, Kelly	
26 Oct	**Ireland 16–15 Argentina**	Adelaide
	T: Quinlan P: O'Gara (2), Humphreyes C: Humphreys	
1 Nov	**Ireland 16–17 Australia**	Melbourne
	T: O'Driscoll P: O'Gara (2) C: O'Gara DG: O'Driscoll	

RWC Pool A Table

	P	W	D	L	F	A	PTS
Australia	4	4	0	0	273	32	18
Ireland	**4**	**3**	**0**	**1**	**141**	**55**	**15**
Argentina	4	2	0	2	140	57	11
Romania	4	1	0	3	65	192	5
Namibia	4	0	0	4	28	310	0

Quarter-final

9 Nov	**Ireland** T: O'Driscoll (2), Maggs C: Humphreys (3)	**21–43 France**	Melbourne

Squad and Coach
Coach: Eddie O'Sullivan
Captain: Keith Wood

Forwards: S. Best (N (r)), S. Byrne (R (r), N (r)), R. Corrigan (R, Ar, A, F), V. Costello (R, Ar, F), S. Easterby (N, Ar, A, F), A. Foley (R, A, F), K. Gleeson (R, A, F), J. Hayes (R (r), N, Ar, A, F), M. Horan (R, N, Ar (r), A (r), F (r)), E. Miller (R (r), N, Ar (r), A, (r), F), D. O'Callaghan (R (r), A (r)), P. O'Connell (R, N, Ar, A, F), M. O'Kelly (R, N, Ar, A, F), A. Quinlan (R (r), N, Ar), K. Wood (R, N, Ar, A, F)

Backs: G. Dempsey (R, N, Ar, A, F), G. Easterby (R (r), N (r), F (r)), D. Hickie (R, N, Ar, A), S. Horgan (R, N, Ar, A, F), D. Humphreys (R, Ar, A (r), F (r)), J. Kelly (R (r), N (r), A (r), F), K. Maggs (R, N, Ar, A, F), B. O'Driscoll (R, N, Ar, A, F), R. O'Gara (R (r), N, Ar (r), A, F), P. Stringer (R, N, Ar, A, F)

Appearances as a replacement marked with (r)

— MONDAY BLUES —

The Irish rugby team must have had a strong sense of déjà vu on their tour of Australia, Tonga and Samoa in the summer of 2003. Having lost to Australia in their opening tour game in Perth, Ireland travelled to Tonga where they beat the home side 40–19. On Tuesday 17 June, three days after the game, the squad departed for Samoa but because they crossed the International Date Line during their flight, they arrived in Samoa on Monday 16 June, the day before they left Tonga.

— (DIS)APPEARANCE —

Blackrock prop Paul Flavin earned one Irish cap when he started against Scotland in the Five Nations of 1997 but a big question mark surrounds another game he was 'capped' in, against France earlier that same season.

After the visitors had scored an injury-time try to put a nice gloss on a 32–15 victory at Lansdowne Road, Nick Popplewell hobbled off injured before the conversion could be taken and he was replaced by an enthusiastic Flavin. But once the conversion had been taken, South African referee Andre Watson blew his final whistle and Flavin was left in rugby purgatory.

Was his 'first cap' a legitimate one? Not according to the rugby statisticians out there, who like to keep these kind of things in check, and even though Flavin was presented with his cap at the banquet after the game, the record books insist that he made only one appearance for Ireland. Which leaves Flavin as quite possibly the only player in international rugby to have a cap taken off him.

— MOST CAPPED —

The most capped Irish players of all time:

Caps	Player	Career
87	Malcolm O'Kelly	1997–
77	Peter Stringer	2000–
75	Girvan Dempsey	1998–
75	Brian O'Driscoll	1999–
74	John Hayes	2000–
73	Ronan O'Gara	2000–
72	David Humphreys	1996–2005
70	Kevin Maggs	1997–2005
69	Mike Gibson	1964–1979
63	Willie John McBride	1962–1975
62	Anthony Foley	1995–2005
61	Fergus Slattery	1970–1984
59	Paddy Johns	1990-2000
58	Phil Orr	1976-1987
58	Keith Wood	1994–2003

— IRISH LEGENDS: PETER CLOHESSY —

Peter Clohessy: the hard man of Irish rugby

Peter Clohessy is without doubt the hard man of Irish rugby. As a prop who could play quite comfortably on either side of the scrum, although he preferred loose head, the Limerick man earned 54 international caps over the course of a nine-year international career but that tally would have been a lot higher had he managed to keep his emotions in check.

On 17 February 1996 in Paris, a game that Ireland lost 45–10 to the rampant home side, Clohessy was caught on camera administering a boot to the head of French second-row Olivier Roumat at a ruck. Whether the shoeing was deliberate or not, the prop was somewhat unfairly vilified by the media who wanted the IRB to take a tough stance against the Young Munster player. Sure enough, Clohessy was given a six-month ban from all levels of rugby in Europe and was expected to hang his head in shame for that period. But that wouldn't have been the player's style. While he did briefly contemplate retiring from the sport for good, an offer from the Queensland Reds caught his interest and during the period he was banned in Europe, Clohessy plied his trade with the Super 12 franchise.

The interesting thing was that when he came back from the southern hemisphere to resume his rugby career, Clohessy seemed much the better player. Not only had he mixed with a different type of prop Down Under, he also trained as a full professional for the first time and it appeared to suit him. He worked his way back into the Irish team by the start of the 1998 Five Nations Championship and from that season onwards, he was one of the first names down on the team sheet until his retirement at the end of the 2002 Six Nations. Any prop who came up against him classed him as one of the most serious operators in world rugby and one of the great pities in Clohessy's career was that he had to withdraw from the 1997 Lions tour to South Africa through injury.

But he had other things to keep him interested. His return from that six-month suspension back in 1997 also coincided with the rise of his province, Munster, in the European game. Clohessy, along with his old friend Mick Galwey, were the leading men in the province's march through Europe at the start of the Millennium. The prop played on the losing side in two Heineken Cup finals for Munster, in 2000 and 2002, but he nearly didn't make it in time for the latter after he suffered serious burns while burning rubbish in his back garden a couple of weeks before the final.

One of Clohessy's greatest regrets was not winning the

Heineken Cup final with Munster but he could be seen celebrating with the squad on the pitch when they finally won their third final against Biarritz in May 2006. Despite all he achieved in his career, the prop still lists the All-Ireland League title won with Young Munster back in 1993 as the highlight of his career. Clohessy now runs an adjoining pub and nightclub in Limerick city called *Clohessy's* and the *Sin-Bin* respectively.

Peter Clohessy
Born: 22 March 1966, Limerick
Club: Young Munster
Caps: 54
Scoring: 20 (4 tries)
Ireland debut: 20 February 1993 v France (Lansdowne Road)

— JOBS FOR THE BOYS —

A selection of the professions of Ireland's internationals:

Player	**Job**
Tom Clifford	Aircraft refueller
Peter Clohessy	Courier
Mick Doyle	Vet
Willie Duggan	Electrical contractor
Eric Elwood	Guinness sales rep
Ciaran Fitzgerald	Army officer
Mike Gibson	Lawyer
Moss Keane	Agricultural inspector
Jackie Kyle	Surgeon
Sean Lynch	Publican
Jim McCoy	RUC officer
John O'Driscoll	Doctor
Tony Ward	Teacher
Keith Wood	Bank official

— IRELAND'S TRIPLE CROWNS: NO. 9, 2007 —

A rusty Ireland batted Wales aside with some difficulty in their opening game at the Millennium Stadium but after England were given a mother and father of a beating at Croke Park at the end of February, Ireland travelled to Edinburgh to try to sew up their ninth Triple Crown. It looked for a good 70 minutes that they would come up just short but Scottish indiscipline in the last ten minutes allowed Ronan O'Gara to slot two penalties to give Ireland a narrow 19–18 win at Murrayfield.

Date	Result	Venue
4 Feb 2007	Ireland 19–9 Wales	Millennium Stadium
11 Feb 2007	Ireland 17–20 France	Croke Park
24 Feb 2007	Ireland 43–13 England	Croke Park
10 Mar 2007	Ireland 19–18 Scotland	Murrayfield
17 Mar 2007	Ireland 51–24 Italy	Stadio Flaminio

— AT LEAST THEY TURNED UP —

After both Scotland and Wales refused to travel to play in Dublin during the 1972 Five Nations Championship because of the growing 'troubles' in Northern Ireland, England were next on Ireland's home schedule at the beginning of the 1973 competition.

It was largely expected that England would not fulfil the fixture but the RFU vowed to send some sort of team to Dublin that year and after various political manoeuvrings, something close to England's best team took the field on 10th February at Lansdowne Road.

As soon as the 15 English players left the tunnel, they were greeted to a resounding cheer from the home crowd and were given a standing ovation for a good five minutes. The home support's good mood continued as Ireland beat the visitors 18–9. At the after-match reception English captain John Pullin commented: "We might not be that good but at least we turn up."

— TRIPLE FROWN —

Ireland have missed out on winning the Triple Crown on the last day of the Championship on 13 separate occasions, 12 times by losing to Wales:

1905 – Wales 10–3 Ireland: A classy Welsh backline proved the difference between the sides despite a huge Irish support at St Helen's. It was a great pity because Ireland had brushed aside both England and Scotland with ease before that.

1911 – Wales 16–0 Ireland: A genuine trouncing, especially considering there were only three points for a try back then. Wales scored three in all and denied Ireland both the Triple Crown, Grand Slam and Championship.

1926 – Wales 11–8 Ireland: Another year where Ireland were on for the Grand Slam and Triple Crown but instead came away with just a share of the Championship. Had Tom Hewitt's last gasp drop goal (worth four points back then) gone over instead of just wide, it would have been a completely different story.

1930 – Wales 12–7 Ireland: A close game at St Helen's but no luck for Ireland despite the best efforts of Paul Murray at out-half.

1931 – Ireland 3–15 Wales: Three tries won this game for Wales as Ireland failed to overturn the hurt of the previous year despite home advantage at Ravenhill.

1936 – Wales 3–0 Ireland: A single penalty from Vivian Jenkins after just 12 minutes settled this one on a tense afternoon at a packed Arms Park.

1939 – Ireland 3–11 Wales: The last Five Nations before the war but a familiar story for Ireland. Wales were just too strong on the day and Ireland would have to wait another eight years to come so close again.

1947 – Wales 6–0 Ireland: After trouncing England 22–0, and scraping past Scotland, Wales stood in the way and it was the same old story, another bad day at St Helen's, Ireland's old bogey ground.

1951 – Wales 3–3 Ireland: The Arms Park was to be Ireland's Waterloo this time around, although they did manage a draw thanks to a Jackie Kyle try. The pity was, had full-back George Norton been available for selection, Ireland would surely have knocked over one of the three simple penalties their stand-in kickers missed.

1965 – Wales 14–8 Ireland: Another depressing day after a promising year. Ray McLoughlin captained an Irish side containing the likes of Tom Kiernan and Willie John McBride but the quality in the visiting ranks just wasn't enough.

1969 – Wales 24–11 Ireland: Home victories against both France and England set Tom Kiernan's men on the road and following a 16–0 victory over Scotland at Murrayfield, things were all set for a Cardiff Arms Park winner-takes-all battle. The thing was that it wasn't so much a battle, more a stroll for a brilliant Wales.

2003 – Ireland 6–42 England: Both sides were in line for both the Triple Crown and Grand Slam in this Sunday fixture but Clive Woodward's side, arguably at the peak of their powers, played some superb power rugby to blow Ireland apart.

2005 – Wales 32–20 Ireland: The fact that Ireland were heading to Wales to win the Triple Crown was almost totally disguised by the fact that the home side were heading for their first Grand Slam in a generation. Tries from Gethin Jenkins and Kevin Morgan won the day for Wales, on a day that Ireland were extremely poor.

— PUT A LID ON IT —

Ireland have only ever played two international fixtures with a stadium roof closed and they've lost both of them. On 1 November 2003, Ireland lost 16–17 to Australia in a Rugby World Cup pool game under the roof of the Telstra Dome in Melbourne and eight days later Eddie O'Sullivan's side lost 21–43 to France at the same venue.

— IRELAND'S RESULTS 1875 TO AUGUST 2007 —

A complete list of Ireland's 562 international results. Of those games, Ireland have won 232, lost 302 and drawn 28. They've scored a total of 7,310 points and conceded 7,660. Ireland's average score over 562 fixtures is a 13–14 defeat.

Key
4NC Four Nations Championship
5NC Five Nations Championship
6NC Six Nations Championship
RWC Rugby World Cup
WCQ World Cup Qualifier

No	Date	Opponents	Trn	Venue	Result
1	15 Feb 1875	England		The Oval	Lost 0 1g,1dg,1t
2	13 Dec 1875	England		Rathmines	Lost 0–1g,1t
3	5 Feb 1877	England		The Oval	Lost 0–2g,2t
4	19 Feb 1877	Scotland		Ormeau	Lost 0–4g,2dg, 2t
5	11 Mar 1878	England		Lansdowne Road	Lost 0–2g,1t
6	17 Feb 1879	Scotland		Ormeau	Lost 0–1g,1dg,1t
7	24 Mar 1879	England		The Oval	Lost 0–2g,1dg,2t
8	30 Jan 1880	England		Lansdowne Road	Lost 1t-1g,1t
9	14 Feb 1880	Scotland		Glasgow	Lost 0–1g,2dg,2t
10	5 Feb 1881	England		Manchester	Lost 0–2g,2t
11	19 Feb 1881	Scotland		Ormeau	Won 1dg-1t
12	28 Jan 1882	Wales		Lansdowne Road	Lost 0–2g,2t
13	6 Feb 1882	England		Lansdowne Road	Drew 2t-2t
14	18 Feb 1882	Scotland		Glasgow	Lost 0–2t
15	5 Feb 1883	England	4NC	Manchester	Lost 1t-1g,3t
16	17 Feb 1883	Scotland	4NC	Ormeau	Lost 0–1g,1t
17	4 Feb 1884	England	4NC	Lansdowne Road	Lost 0–1g
18	16 Feb 1884	Scotland	4NC	Edinburgh	Lost 1t-2g,2t
19	12 April 1884	Wales	4NC	Cardiff Arms Park	Lost 0–1dg,2t
20	7 Feb 1885	England	4NC	Manchester	Lost 1t-2t
21	21 Feb 1885	Scotland	4NC	Ormeau	Lost 0–1g,2t
22	7 Mar 1885	Scotland	4NC	Edinburgh	Lost 0–3g,2dg,2t
23	6 Feb 1886	England	4NC	Lansdowne Road	Lost 0–1t
24	20 Feb 1886	Scotland	4NC	Edinburgh	Lost 0–3g,1dg,2t
25	5 Feb 1887	England	4NC	Lansdowne Road	Won 2g-0
26	19 Feb 1887	Scotland	4NC	Ormeau	Lost 0–1g,1dg,1t

27	12 Mar 1887	Wales	4NC	Birkenhead	Lost 3t-1dg,1t
28	3 Mar 1888	Wales	4NC	Lansdowne Road	Won 1g,1dg,1t-0
29	10 Mar 1888	Scotland	4NC	Edinburgh	Lost 0–1g
30	16 Feb 1889	Scotland	4NC	Ormeau	Lost 0–1dg
31	2 Mar 1889	Wales	4NC	Swansea	Won 2t-0
32	22 Feb 1890	Scotland	4NC	Edinburgh	Lost 0–1dg,1t
33	1 Mar 1890	Wales	4NC	Lansdowne Road	Drew 1g-1g
34	15 Mar 1890	England	4NC	Blackheath	Lost 0–3t
35	7 Feb 1891	England	4NC	Lansdowne Road	Lost 0–9
36	21 Feb 1891	Scotland	4NC	Ballynafeigh	Lost 0–14
37	7 Mar 1891	Wales	4NC	Llanelli	Lost 4–6
38	6 Feb 1892	England	4NC	Manchester	Lost 0–7
39	20 Feb 1892	Scotland	4NC	Edinburgh	Lost 0–2
40	5 Mar 1892	Wales	4NC	Lansdowne Road	Lost 0–9
41	4 Feb 1893	England	4NC	Lansdowne Road	Lost 0–4
42	18 Feb 1893	Scotland	4NC	Ballynafeigh	Drew 0–0
43	11 Mar 1893	Wales	4NC	Llanelli	Lost 0–2
44	3 Feb 1894	England	4NC	Blackheath	Won 7–5
45	24 Feb 1894	Scotland	4NC	Lansdowne Road	Won 5–0
46	10 Mar 1894	Wales	4NC	Ballynafeigh	Won 3–0
47	2 Feb 1895	England	4NC	Lansdowne Road	Lost 3–6
48	2 Mar 1895	Scotland	4NC	Edinburgh	Lost 0–6
49	16 Mar 1895	Wales	4NC	Cardiff Arms Park	Lost 3–5
50	1 Feb 1896	England	4NC	Leeds	Won 10–4
51	15 Feb 1896	Scotland	4NC	Lansdowne Road	Drew 0–0
52	14 Mar 1896	Wales	4NC	Lansdowne Road	Won 8–4
53	6 Feb 1897	England	4NC	Lansdowne Road	Won 13–9
54	20 Feb 1897	Scotland	4NC	Edinburgh	Lost 3–8
55	5 Feb 1898	England	4NC	Richmond	Won 9–6
56	19 Feb 1898	Scotland	4NC	Balmoral	Lost 0–8
57	19 Mar 1898	Wales	4NC	Limerick	Lost 3–11
58	4 Feb 1899	England	4NC	Lansdowne Road	Won 6–0
59	18 Feb 1899	Scotland	4NC	Inverleith	Won 9–3
60	18 Mar 1899	Wales	4NC	Cardiff Arms Park	Won 3–0
61	3 Feb 1900	England	4NC	Richmond	Lost 4–15
62	24 Feb 1900	Scotland	4NC	Lansdowne Road	Drew 0–0
63	17 Mar 1900	Wales	4NC	Balmoral	Lost 0–3
64	9 Feb 1901	England	4NC	Lansdowne Road	Won 10–6
65	23 Feb 1901	Scotland	4NC	Inverleith	Lost 5–9
66	16 Mar 1901	Wales	4NC	Swansea	Lost 9–10

67	8 Feb 1902	England	4NC	Welford Road	Lost 3–6
68	22 Feb 1902	Scotland	4NC	Balmoral	Won 5–0
69	8 Mar 1902	Wales	4NC	Lansdowne Road	Lost 0–15
70	14 Feb 1903	England	4NC	Lansdowne Road	Won 6–0
71	28 Feb 1903	Scotland	4NC	Inverleith	Lost 0–3
72	14 Mar 1903	Wales	4NC	Cardiff Arms Park	Lost 0–18
73	13 Feb 1904	England	4NC	Blackheath	Lost 0–19
74	27 Feb 1904	Scotland	4NC	Lansdowne Road	Lost 3–19
75	12 Mar 1904	Wales	4NC	Balmoral	Won 14–12
76	11 Feb 1905	England	4NC	Cork	Won 17–3
77	25 Feb 1905	Scotland	4NC	Inverleith	Won 11–5
78	11 Mar 1905	Wales	4NC	Swansea	Lost 3–10
79	25 Nov 1905	New Zealand		Lansdowne Road	Lost 0–15
80	10 Feb 1906	England	4NC	Welford Road	Won 16–6
81	24 Feb 1906	Scotland	4NC	Lansdowne Road	Lost 6–13
82	10 Mar 1906	Wales	4NC	Balmoral	Won 11–6
83	24 Nov 1906	South Africa		Ravenhill	Lost 12–15
84	9 Feb 1907	England	4NC	Lansdowne Road	Won 17–9
85	23 Feb 1907	Scotland	4NC	Inverleith	Lost 3–15
86	9 Mar 1907	Wales	4NC	Cardiff Arms Park	Lost 0–29
87	8 Feb 1908	England	4NC	Richmond	Lost 3–13
88	29 Feb 1908	Scotland	4NC	Lansdowne Road	Won 16–11
89	14 Mar 1908	Wales	4NC	Balmoral	Lost 5–11
90	13 Feb 1909	England	4NC	Lansdowne Road	Lost 5–11
91	27 Feb 1909	Scotland	4NC	Inverleith	Lost 3–9
92	13 Mar 1909	Wales	4NC	Swansea	Lost 5–18
93	20 Mar 1909	France		Lansdowne Road	Won 19–8
94	12 Feb 1910	England	5NC	Twickenham	Drew 0–0
95	26 Feb 1910	Scotland	5NC	Balmoral	Lost 0–14
96	12 Mar 1910	Wales	5NC	Lansdowne Road	Lost 3–19
97	28 Mar 1910	France	5NC	Parc des Princes	Won 8–3
98	11 Feb 1911	England	5NC	Lansdowne Road	Won 3–0
99	25 Feb 1911	Scotland	5NC	Inverleith	Won 16–10
100	11 Mar 1911	Wales	5NC	Cardiff Arms Park	Lost 0–16
101	25 Mar 1911	France	5NC	Cork	Won 25–5
102	1 Jan 1912	France	5NC	Parc des Princes	Won 11–6
103	10 Feb 1912	England	5NC	Twickenham	Lost 0–15
104	24 Feb 1912	Scotland	5NC	Lansdowne Road	Won 10–8

105	9 Mar 1912	Wales	5NC	Balmoral	Won 12–5
106	30 Nov 1912	South Africa		Lansdowne Road	Lost 0–38
107	8 Feb 1913	England	5NC	Lansdowne Road	Lost 4–15
108	22 Feb 1913	Scotland	5NC	Inverleith	Lost 14–29
109	9 Mar 1913	Wales	5NC	Swansea	Lost 13–16
110	24 Mar 1913	France	5NC	Cork	Won 24–0
111	1 Jan 1914	France	5NC	Parc des Princes	Won 8–6
112	14 Feb 1914	England	5NC	Twickenham	Lost 12–17
113	28 Feb 1914	Scotland	5NC	Lansdowne Road	Won 6–0
114	14 Mar 1914	Wales	5NC	Balmoral	Lost 3–11
115	14 Feb 1920	England	5NC	Lansdowne Road	Lost 11–14
116	28 Feb 1920	Scotland	5NC	Inverleith	Lost 0–19
117	13 Mar 1920	Wales	5NC	Cardiff Arms Park	Lost 4–28
118	3 April 1920	France	5NC	Lansdowne Road	Lost 7–15
119	12 Feb 1921	England	5NC	Twickenham	Lost 0–15
120	26 Feb 1921	Scotland	5NC	Lansdowne Road	Won 9–8
121	12 Mar 1921	Wales	5NC	Balmoral	Lost 0–6
122	9 April 1921	France	5NC	Stade Colombes	Lost 10–20
123	11 Feb 1922	England	5NC	Lansdowne Road	Lost 3–12
124	25 Feb 1922	Scotland	5NC	Inverleith	Lost 3–6
125	11 Mar 1922	Wales	5NC	Swansea	Lost 5–11
126	9 April 1922	France	5NC	Lansdowne Road	Won 8–3
127	10 Feb 1923	England	5NC	Welford Road	Lost 5–23
128	24 Feb 1923	Scotland	5NC	Lansdowne Road	Lost 3–13
129	10 Mar 1923	Wales	5NC	Lansdowne Road	Won 5–4
130	14 April 1923	France	5NC	Stade Colombes	Lost 8–14
131	26 Jan 1924	France	5NC	Lansdowne Road	Won 6–0
132	9 Feb 1924	England	5NC	Ravenhill	Lost 3–14
133	23 Feb 1924	Scotland	5NC	Inverleith	Lost 8–13
134	8 Mar 1924	Wales	5NC	Cardiff Arms Park	Won 13–10
135	1 Nov 1924	New Zealand		Lansdowne Road	Lost 0–6
136	1 Jan 1925	France	5NC	Stade Colombes	Won 9–3
137	14 Feb 1925	England	5NC	Twickenham	Drew 6–6
138	28 Feb 1925	Scotland	5NC	Lansdowne Road	Lost 8–14
139	14 Mar 1925	Wales	5NC	Ravenhill	Won 19–3
140	23 Jan 1926	France	5NC	Ravenhill	Won 11–0
141	13 Feb 1926	England	5NC	Lansdowne Road	Won 19–15
142	27 Feb 1926	Scotland	5NC	Murrayfield	Won 3–0

143	13 Mar 1926	Wales	5NC	Swansea	Lost 8–11
144	1 Jan 1927	France	5NC	Stade Colombes	Won 8–3
145	12 Feb 1927	England	5NC	Twickenham	Lost 6–8
146	26 Feb 1927	Scotland	5NC	Lansdowne Road	Won 6–0
147	12 Mar 1927	Wales	5NC	Lansdowne Road	Won 19–9
148	28 Jan 1928	France	5NC	Ravenhill	Won 12–8
149	11 Feb 1928	England	5NC	Lansdowne Road	Lost 6–7
150	25 Feb 1928	Scotland	5NC	Murrayfield	Won 13–5
151	10 Mar 1928	Wales	5NC	Cardiff Arms Park	Won 13–10
152	31 Dec 1928	France	5NC	Stade Colombes	Won 6–0
153	9 Feb 1929	England	5NC	Twickenham	Won 6–5
154	23 Feb 1929	Scotland	5NC	Lansdowne Road	Lost 7–16
155	9 Mar 1929	Wales	5NC	Ravenhill	Drew 5–5
156	25 Jan 1930	France	5NC	France	Lost 0–5
157	8 Feb 1930	England	5NC	Lansdowne Road	Won 4–3
158	22 Feb 1930	Scotland	5NC	Murrayfield	Won 14–11
159	8 Mar 1930	Wales	5NC	Swansea	Lost 7–12
160	1 Jan 1931	France	5NC	Stade Colombes	Lost 0–3
161	14 Feb 1931	England	5NC	Twickenham	Won 6–5
162	28 Feb 1931	Scotland	5NC	Lansdowne Road	Won 8–5
163	14 Mar 1931	Wales	5NC	Ravenhill	Lost 3–15
164	19 Dec 1931	South Africa		Lansdowne Road	Lost 3–8
165	13 Feb 1932	England	4NC	Lansdowne Road	Lost 8–11
166	27 Feb 1932	Scotland	4NC	Murrayfield	Won 20–8
167	12 Mar 1932	Wales	4NC	Cardiff Arms Park	Won 12–10
168	11 Feb 1933	England	4NC	Twickenham	Lost 6–17
169	11 Mar 1933	Wales	4NC	Ravenhill	Won 10–5
170	1 April 1933	Scotland	4NC	Lansdowne Road	Lost 6–8
171	10 Feb 1934	England	4NC	Lansdowne Road	Lost 3–13
172	24 Feb 1934	Scotland	4NC	Murrayfield	Lost 9–16
173	10t Mar 1934	Wales	4NC	Swansea	Lost 0–13
174	9 Feb 1935	England	4NC	Twickenham	Lost 3–14
175	23 Feb 1935	Scotland	4NC	Lansdowne Road	Won 12–5
176	9 Mar 1935	Wales	4NC	Ravenhill	Won 9–3
177	7 Dec 1935	New Zealand		Lansdowne Road	Lost 9–17
178	8 Feb 1936	England	4NC	Lansdowne Road	Won 6–3
179	22 Feb 1936	Scotland	4NC	Murrayfield	Won 10–4
180	14 Mar 1936	Wales	4NC	Cardiff Arms Park	Lost 0–3

181	13 Feb 1937	England	4NC	Twickenham	Lost 8–9
182	27 Feb 1937	Scotland	4NC	Lansdowne Road	Won 11–4
183	3 April 1937	Wales	4NC	Ravenhill	Won 5–3
184	12 Feb 1938	England	4NC	Lansdowne Road	Lost 14–36
185	26 Feb 1938	Scotland	4NC	Murrayfield	Lost 14–23
186	11 Feb 1939	England	4NC	Twickenham	Won 5–0
187	25 Feb 1939	Scotland	4NC	Lansdowne Road	Won 12–3
188	11 Mar 1939	Wales	4NC	Ravenhill	Lost 0–7
189	25 Jan 1947	France	5NC	Lansdowne Road	Lost 8–12
190	8 Feb 1947	England	5NC	Lansdowne Road	Won 22–0
191	22 Feb 1947	Scotland	5NC	Murrayfield	Won 3–0
192	29 Mar 1947	Wales	5NC	Swansea	Lost 0–6
193	6 Dec 1947	Australia		Lansdowne Road	Lost 3–16
194	1 Jan 1948	France	5NC	Stade Colombes	Won 13–6
195	14 Feb 1948	England	5NC	Twickenham	Won 11–10
196	28 Feb 1948	Scotland	5NC	Lansdowne Road	Won 6–0
197	13 Mar 1948	Wales	5NC	Ravenhill	Won 6–3
198	29 Jan 1949	France	5NC	Lansdowne Road	Lost 9–16
199	12 Feb 1949	England	5NC	Lansdowne Road	Won 14–5
200	26 Feb 1949	Scotland	5NC	Murrayfield	Won 13–3
201	12 Mar 1949	Wales	5NC	Swansea	Won 5–0
202	28 Jan 1950	France	5NC	Stade Colombes	Drew 3–3
203	11 Feb 1950	England	5NC	Twickenham	Lost 0–3
204	25 Feb 1950	Scotland	5NC	Lansdowne Road	Won 21–0
205	11 Mar 1950	Wales	5NC	Ravenhill	Lost 3–6
206	27 Jan 1951	France	5NC	Lansdowne Road	Won 9–8
207	10 Feb 1951	England	5NC	Lansdowne Road	Won 3–0
208	24 Feb 1951	Scotland	5NC	Murrayfield	Won 6–5
209	10 Mar 1951	Wales	5NC	Cardiff Arms Park	Drew 3–3
210	8 Dec 1951	South Africa		Lansdowne Road	Lost 5–17
211	26 Jan 1952	France	5NC	Stade Colombes	Won 11–8
212	23 Feb 1952	Scotland	5NC	Lansdowne Road	Won 12–8
213	8 Mar 1952	Wales	5NC	Lansdowne Road	Lost 3–14
214	29 Mar 1952	England	5NC	Twickenham	Lost 0–3
215	24 Aug 1952	Argentina		Buenos Aires	Drew 3–3
216	31 Aug 1952	Argentina		Buenos Aires	Won 6–0
217	24 Jan 1953	France	5NC	Ravenhill	Won 16–3
218	14 Feb 1953	England	5NC	Lansdowne Road	Drew 9–9
219	28 Feb 1953	Scotland	5NC	Murrayfield	Won 26–8

220	14 Mar 1953	Wales	5NC	Swansea	Lost 3–5
221	9 Jan 1954	New Zealand		Lansdowne Road	Lost 3–14
222	23 Jan 1954	France	5NC	Stade Colombes	Lost 0–8
223	13 Feb 1954	England	5NC	Twickenham	Lost 3–14
224	27 Feb 1954	Scotland	5NC	Ravenhill	Won 6–0
225	13 Mar 1954	Wales	5NC	Lansdowne Road	Lost 9–12
226	22 Jan 1955	France	5NC	Lansdowne Road	Lost 3–5
227	12 Feb 1955	England	5NC	Lansdowne Road	Drew 6–6
228	26 Feb 1955	Scotland	5NC	Murrayfield	Lost 3–12
229	12 Mar 1955	Wales	5NC	Cardiff Arms Park	Lost 3–21
230	28 Jan 1956	France	5NC	Stade Colombes	Lost 8–14
231	11 Feb 1986	England	5NC	Twickenham	Lost 0–20
232	25 Feb 1956	Scotland	5NC	Lansdowne Road	Won 14–10
233	10 Mar 1956	Wales	5NC	Lansdowne Road	Won 11–3
234	26 Jan 1957	France	5NC	Lansdowne Road	Won 11–6
235	9 Feb 1957	England	5NC	Lansdowne Road	Lost 0–6
236	23 Feb 1957	Scotland	5NC	Murrayfield	Won 5–3
237	9 Mar 1957	Wales	5NC	Cardiff Arms Park	Lost 5–6
238	18 Jan 1958	Australia	5NC	Lansdowne Road	Won 9–6
239	8 Feb 1958	England	5NC	Twickenham	Lost 0–6
240	1 Mar 1958	Scotland	5NC	Lansdowne Road	Won 12–6
241	15 Mar 1958	Wales	5NC	Lansdowne Road	Lost 6–9
242	19 April 1958	France	5NC	Stade Colombes	Lost 6–11
243	14 Feb 1959	England	5NC	Lansdowne Road	Lost 0–3
244	28 Feb 1959	Scotland	5NC	Murrayfield	Won 8–3
245	14 Mar 1959	Wales	5NC	Cardiff Arms Park	Lost 6–8
246	18 April 1959	France	5NC	Lansdowne Road	Won 9–5
247	13 Feb 1960	England	5NC	Twickenham	Lost 5–8
248	27 Feb 1960	Scotland	5NC	Lansdowne Road	Lost 5–6
249	12 Mar 1960	Wales	5NC	Lansdowne Road	Lost 9–10
250	9 April 1960	France	5NC	Stade Colombes	Lost 6–23
251	17 Dec 1960	South Africa		Lansdowne Road	Lost 3–8
252	11 Feb 1961	England	5NC	Lansdowne Road	Won 11–8
253	25 Feb 1961	Scotland	5NC	Murrayfield	Lost 8–16
254	11 Mar 1961	Wales	5NC	Cardiff Arms Park	Lost 0–9
255	13 May 1961	South Africa	5NC	Cape Town	Lost 8–24
256	10 Feb 1962	England	5NC	Twickenham	Lost 0–16

257	24 Feb 1962	Scotland	5NC	Lansdowne Road	Lost 6–20
258	14 April 1962	France	5NC	Stade Colombes	Lost 0–11
259	17 Nov 1962	Wales	5NC	Lansdowne Road	Drew 3–3
260	26 Jan 1963	France	5NC	Lansdowne Road	Lost 5–24
261	9 Feb 1963	England	5NC	Lansdowne Road	Drew 0–0
262	23 Feb 1963	Scotland	5NC	Murrayfield	Lost 0–3
263	9 Mar 1963	Wales	5NC	Cardiff Arms Park	Won 14–6
264	7 Dec 1963	New Zealand		Lansdowne Road	Lost 5–6
265	8 Feb 1964	England	5NC	Twickenham	Won 18–5
266	22 Feb 1964	Scotland	5NC	Lansdowne Road	Lost 3–6
267	7 Mar 1964	Wales	5NC	Lansdowne Road	Lost 6–15
268	11 April 1964	France	5NC	Stade Colombes	Lost 6–27
269	23 Jan 1965	France	5NC	Lansdowne Road	Drew 3–3
270	13 Feb 1965	England	5NC	Lansdowne Road	Won 5–0
271	27 Feb 1965	Scotland	5NC	Murrayfield	Won 16–6
272	13 Mar 1965	Wales	5NC	Cardiff Arms Park	Lost 8–14
273	10 April 1965	South Africa		Lansdowne Road	Won 9–6
274	29 Jan 1966	France	5NC	Stade Colombes	Lost 6–11
275	12 Feb 1966	England	5NC	Twickenham	Drew 6–6
276	26 Feb 1966	Scotland	5NC	Lansdowne Road	Lost 3–11
277	12 Mar 1966	Wales	5NC	Lansdowne Road	Won 9–6
278	21 Jan 1967	Australia		Lansdowne Road	Won 15–8
279	11 Feb 1967	England	5NC	Lansdowne Road	Lost 3–8
280	25 Feb 1967	Scotland	5NC	Murrayfield	Won 5–3
281	11 Mar 1967	Wales	5NC	Cardiff Arms Park	Won 3–0
282	15 April 1967	France	5NC	Lansdowne Road	Lost 6–11
283	13 May 1967	Australia	5NC	Sydney	Won 11–5
284	27 Jan 1968	France	5NC	Stade Colombes	Lost 6–16
285	10 Feb 1968	England	5NC	Twickenham	Drew 9–9
286	24 Feb 1968	Scotland	5NC	Lansdowne Road	Won 14–6
287	9 Mar 1968	Wales	5NC	Lansdowne Road	Won 9–6
288	26 Oct 1968	Australia		Lansdowne Road	Won 10–3
289	25 Jan 1969	France	5NC	Lansdowne Road	Won 17–9
290	8 Feb 1969	England	5NC	Lansdowne Road	Won 17–15
291	22 Feb 1969	Scotland	5NC	Murrayfield	Won 16–0
292	8 Mar 1969	Wales	5NC	Cardiff Arms Park	Lost 11–24
293	10 Jan 1970	South Africa		Lansdowne Road	Drew 8–8

294	24 Jan 1970	France	5NC	Stade Colombes	Lost 0–8
295	14 Jan 1970	England	5NC	Twickenham	Lost 3–9
296	28 Feb 1970	Scotland	5NC	Lansdowne Road	Won 16–11
297	14 Mar 1970	Wales	5NC	Lansdowne Road	Won 14–0
298	13 Sept 1970	Argentina		Buenos Aires	Lost 3–8
299	20 Sept 1970	Argentina		Buenos Aires	Lost 3–6
300	30 Jan 1971	France	5NC	Lansdowne Road	Drew 9–9
301	13 Feb 1971	England	5NC	Lansdowne Road	Lost 6–9
302	27 Feb 1971	Scotland	5NC	Murrayfield	Won 17–5
303	13 Mar 1971	Wales	5NC	Cardiff Arms Park	Lost 9–23
304	29 Jan 1972	France	5NC	Stade Colombes	Won 14–9
305	12 Feb 1972	England	5NC	Twickenham	Won 16–12
306	29 April 1972	France	5NC	Lansdowne Road	Won 24–14
307	20 Jan 1973	New Zealand		Lansdowne Road	Drew 10–10
308	10 Feb 1973	England	5NC	Lansdowne Road	Won 18–9
309	24 Feb 1973	Scotland	5NC	Murrayfield	Lost 14–19
310	10 Mar 1973	Wales	5NC	Cardiff Arms Park	Lost 12–16
311	14 April 1973	France	5NC	Lansdowne Road	Won 6–4
312	10 Nov 1973	Argentina		Lansdowne Road	Won 21–8
313	19 Jan 1974	France	5NC	Parc des Princes	Lost 6–9
314	2 Feb 1974	Wales	5NC	Lansdowne Road	Drew 9–9
315	16 Feb 1974	England	5NC	Twickenham	Won 26–21
316	2 Mar 1974	Scotland	5NC	Lansdowne Road	Won 9–6
317	23 Nov 1974	New Zealand		Lansdowne Road	Lost 6–15
318	18 Jan 1975	England	5NC	Lansdowne Road	Won 12–9
319	1 Feb 1975	Scotland	5NC	Murrayfield	Lost 13–20
320	1 Mar 1975	France	5NC	Lansdowne Road	Won 25–6
321	15 Mar 1975	Wales	5NC	Cardiff Arms Park	Lost 4–32
322	17 Jan 1976	Australia		Lansdowne Road	Lost 10–20
323	7 Feb 1976	France	5NC	Parc des Princes	Lost 3–26
324	21 Feb 1976	Wales	5NC	Lansdowne Road	Lost 9–34
325	6 Mar 1976	England	5NC	Twickenham	Won 13–12
326	20 Mar 1976	Scotland	5NC	Lansdowne Road	Lost 6–15
327	5 June 1976	New Zealand		Wellington	Lost 3–11
328	15 Jan 1977	Wales	5NC	Cardiff Arms Park	Lost 9–25
329	5 Feb 1977	England	5NC	Lansdowne Road	Lost 0–4
330	19 Feb 1977	Scotland	5NC	Murrayfield	Lost 18–21

331	19 Mar 1977	France	5NC	Lansdowne Road	Lost 6–15
332	21 Jan 1978	Scotland	5NC	Lansdowne Road	Won 12–9
333	18 Feb 1978	France	5NC	Parc des Princes	Lost 9–10
334	4 Mar 1978	Wales	5NC	Lansdowne Road	Lost 16–20
335	18 Mar 1978	England	5NC	Twickenham	Lost 9–15
336	4 Nov 1978	New Zealand		Lansdowne Road	Lost 6–10
337	20 Jan 1979	France	5NC	Lansdowne Road	Drew 9–9
338	3 Feb 1979	Wales	5NC	Cardiff Arms Park	Lost 21–24
339	17 Feb 1979	England	5NC	Lansdowne Road	Won 12–7
340	3 Mar 1979	Scotland	5NC	Murrayfield	Drew 11–11
341	3 June 1979	Australia		Brisbane	Won 27–12
342	16 June 1979	Australia		Sydney	Won 9–3
343	19 Jan 1980	England	5NC	Twickenham	Lost 9–24
344	2 Feb 1980	Scotland	5NC	Lansdowne Road	Won 22–15
345	1 Mar 1980	France	5NC	Parc des Princes	Lost 18–19
346	15 Mar 1980	Wales	5NC	Lansdowne Road	Won 21–7
347	7 Feb 1981	France	5NC	Lansdowne Road	Lost 13–19
348	21 Feb 1981	Wales	5NC	Cardiff Arms Park	Lost 8–9
349	7 Mar 1981	England	5NC	Lansdowne Road	Lost 6–10
350	21 Mar 1981	Scotland	5NC	Murrayfield	Lost 9–10
351	30 May 1981	South Africa		Cape Town	Lost 15–23
352	6 June 1981	South Africa		Durban	Lost 10–12
353	21 Nov 1981	Australia		Lansdowne Road	Lost 12–16
354	23 Jan 1982	Wales	5NC	Lansdowne Road	Won 20–12
355	6 Feb 1982	England	5NC	Twickenham	Won 16–15
356	20 Feb 1982	Scotland	5NC	Lansdowne Road	Won 21–12
357	20 Mar 1982	France	5NC	Parc des Princes	Lost 9–22
358	15 Jan 1983	Scotland	5NC	Murrayfield	Won 15–13
359	19 Feb 1983	France	5NC	Lansdowne Road	Won 22–16
360	5 Mar 1983	Wales	5NC	Cardiff Arms Park	Lost 9–23
361	19 Mar 1983	England	5NC	Lansdowne Road	Won 25–15
362	21 Jan 1984	France	5NC	Parc des Princes	Lost 12–25
363	4 Feb 1984	Wales	5NC	Lansdowne Road	Lost 9–18
364	18 Feb 1984	England	5NC	Twickenham	Lost 9–12
365	3 March 1984	Scotland	5NC	Lansdowne Road	Lost 9–32
366	10 Nov 1984	Australia		Lansdowne Road	Lost 9–16
367	2 Feb 1985	Scotland	5NC	Murrayfield	Won 18–15

368	2 Mar 1985	France	5NC	Lansdowne Road	Drew 15–15
369	16 Mar 1985	Wales	5NC	Cardiff Arms Park	Won 21–9
370	30 Mar 1985	England	5NC	Lansdowne Road	Won 13–10
371	1 Feb 1986	France	5NC	Parc des Princes	Lost 9–29
372	15 Feb 1986	Wales	5NC	Lansdowne Road	Lost 12–19
373	1 Mar 1986	England	5NC	Twickenham	Lost 20–25
374	15 Mar 1986	Scotland	5NC	Lansdowne Road	Lost 9–10
375	1 Nov 1986	Romania		Lansdowne Road	Won 60–0
376	7 Feb 1987	England	5NC	Lansdowne Road	Won 17–0
377	21 Feb 1987	Scotland	5NC	Murrayfield	Lost 12–16
378	21 Mar 1987	France	5NC	Lansdowne Road	Lost 13–19
379	4 April 1987	Wales	5NC	Cardiff Arms Park	Won 15–11
380	25 May 1987	Wales	RWC	Wellington	Lost 6–13
381	30 May 1987	Canada	RWC	Dunedin	Won 46–19
382	3 June 1987	Tonga	RWC	Brisbane	Won 32–9
383	7 June 1987	Australia	RWC	Sydney	Lost 15–33
384	16 Jan 1988	Scotland	5NC	Lansdowne Road	Won 22–18
385	20 Feb 1988	France	5NC	Parc des Princes	Lost 6–25
386	5 Mar 1988	Wales	5NC	Lansdowne Road	Lost 9–12
387	19 Mar 1988	England	5NC	Twickenham	Lost 3–35
388	23 April 1988	England	5NC	Lansdowne Road	Lost 10–21
389	29 Oct 1988	Samoa		Lansdowne Road	Won 49–22
390	31 Dec 1988	Italy		Lansdowne Road	Won 31–15
391	21 Jan 1989	France	5NC	Lansdowne Road	Lost 21–26
392	4 Feb 1989	Wales	5NC	Cardiff Arms Park	Won 19–13
393	18 Feb 1989	England	5NC	Lansdowne Road	Lost 3–16
394	4 Mar 1989	Scotland	5NC	Murrayfield	Lost 21–37
395	18 Nov 1989	New Zealand		Lansdowne Road	Lost 6–23
396	20 Jan 1990	England	5NC	Twickenham	Lost 0–23
397	3 Feb 1990	Scotland	5NC	Lansdowne Road	Lost 10–13
398	3 Mar 1990	France	5NC	Parc des Princes	Lost 12–31
399	24 Mar 1990	Wales	5NC	Lansdowne Road	Won 14–8
400	27 Oct 1990	Argentina		Lansdowne Road	Won 20–18
401	2 Feb 1991	France	5NC	Lansdowne Road	Lost 13–21
402	16 Feb 1991	Wales	5NC	Cardiff Arms Park	Drew 21–21
403	2 Mar 1991	England	5NC	Lansdowne Road	Lost 7–16
404	16 Mar 1991	Scotland	5NC	Murrayfield	Lost 25–28
405	20 July 1991	Namibia		Windhoek	Lost 6–15
406	27 July 1991	Namibia		Windhoek	Lost 15–26

407	6 Oct 1991	Zimbabwe	RWC	Lansdowne Road	Won 55–11
408	9 Oct 1991	Japan	RWC	Lansdowne Road	Won 32–16
409	12 Oct 1991	Scotland	RWC	Murrayfield	Lost 15–24
410	20 Oct 1991	Australia	RWC	Lansdowne Road	Lost 18–19
411	18 Jan 1992	Wales	5NC	Lansdowne Road	Lost 15–16
412	1 Feb 1992	England	5NC	Twickenham	Lost 9–38
413	15 Feb 1992	Scotland	5NC	Lansdowne Road	Lost 10–18
414	21 Mar 1992	France	5NC	Parc des Princes	Lost 12–44
415	30 May 1992	New Zealand		Dunedin	Lost 21–24
416	6 June 1992	New Zealand		Wellington	Lost 6–59
417	31 Oct 1992	Australia		Lansdowne Road	Lost 17–42
418	16 Jan 1993	Scotland	5NC	Murrayfield	Lost 3–15
419	20 Feb 1993	France	5NC	Lansdowne Road	Lost 6–21
420	6 Mar 1993	Wales	5NC	Cardiff Arms Park	Won 19–14
421	20 Mar 1993	England	5NC	Lansdowne Road	Won 17–3
422	13 Nov 1993	Romania		Lansdowne Road	Won 25–3
423	15 Jan 1994	France	5NC	Parc des Princes	Lost 15–35
424	5 Feb 1994	Wales	5NC	Lansdowne Road	Lost 15–17
425	19 Feb 1994	England	5NC	Twickenham	Won 13–12
426	5 Mar 1994	Scotland	5NC	Lansdowne Road	Drew 6–6
427	5 June 1994	Australia		Brisbane	Lost 13–33
428	11 June 1994	Australia		Sydney	Lost 18–32
429	5 Nov 1994	USA		Lansdowne Road	Won 16–15
430	21 Jan 1995	England	5NC	Lansdowne Road	Lost 8–20
431	4 Feb 1995	Scotland	5NC	Murrayfield	Lost 13–26
432	4 Mar 1995	France	5NC	Lansdowne Road	Lost 7–25
433	18 Mar 1995	Wales	5NC	Cardiff Arms Park	Won 16–12
434	6 May 1995	Italy		Treviso	Lost 12–22
435	27 May 1995	New Zealand	RWC	Ellis Park	Lost 19–43
436	31 May 1995	Japan	RWC	Bloemfontein	Won 50–28
437	4 June 1995	Wales	RWC	Ellis Park	Won 24–23
438	10 June 1995	France	RWC	Durban	Lost 12–36
439	18 Nov 1995	Fiji	RWC	Lansdowne Road	Won 44–8
440	6 Jan 1996	USA		Atlanta	Won 25–18
441	20 Jan 1996	Scotland	5NC	Lansdowne Road	Lost 10–16
442	17 Feb 1996	France	5NC	Parc des Princes	Lost 10–45
443	2 Mar 1996	Wales	5NC	Lansdowne Road	Won 30–17

444	16 Mar 1996	England	5NC	Twickenham	Lost 15–28
445	12 Nov 1996	Samoa		Lansdowne Road	Lost 25–40
446	23 Nov 1996	Australia		Lansdowne Road	Lost 12–22
447	4 Jan 1997	Italy		Landowne Road	Lost 29–37
448	18 Jan 1997	France	5NC	Lansdowne Road	Lost 15–32
449	1 Feb 1997	Wales	5NC	Cardiff Arms Park	Won 26–25
450	15 Feb 1997	England	5NC	Lansdowne Road	Lost 6–46
451	1 Mar 1997	Scotland	5NC	Murrayfield	Lost 10–38
452	15 Nov 1997	New Zealand		Lansdowne Road	Lost 16–63
453	30 Nov 1997	Canada		Lansdowne Road	Won 33–11
454	20 Dec 1997	Italy		Bologna	Lost 22–37
455	7 Feb 1998	Scotland	5NC	Lansdowne Road	Lost 16–17
456	7 Mar 1998	France	5NC	Stade de France	Lost 16–18
457	21 Mar 1998	Wales	5NC	Lansdowne Road	Lost 21–30
458	4 April 1998	England	5NC	Twickenham	Lost 17–35
459	13 June 1998	South Africa		Bloemfontein	Lost 13–37
460	20 June 1998	South Africa		Pretoria	Lost 0–33
461	14 Nov 1998	Georgia	RWQ	Lansdowne Road	Won 70–0
462	21 Nov 1998	Romania	RWQ	Lansdowne Road	Won 53–35
463	28 Nov 1998	South Africa		Lansdowne Road	Lost 13–27
464	6 Feb 1999	France	5N	Lansdowne Road	Lost 9–10
465	20 Feb 1999	Wales	5N	Wembley	Won 29–23
466	6 Mar 1999	England	5N	Lansdowne Road	Lost 15–27
467	20 Mar 1999	Scotland	5N	Murrayfield	Lost 13–30
468	10 April 1999	Italy		Lansdowne Road	Won 39–30
469	12 June 1999	Australia		Brisbane	Lost 10–46
470	19 June 1999	Australia		Perth	Lost 26–32
471	28 Aug 1999	Argentina		Lansdowne Road	Won 32–24
472	2 Oct 1999	USA	RWC	Lansdowne Road	Won 53–8
473	10 Oct 1999	Australia	RWC	Lansdowne Road	Lost 3–23
474	15 Oct 1999	Romania	RWC	Lansdowne Road	Won 44–14
475	20 Oct 1999	Argentina	RWC	Lens	Lost 24–28
476	5 Feb 2000	England	6NC	Twickenham	Lost 18–50
477	19 Feb 2000	Scotland	6NC	Lansdowne Road	Won 44–22
478	4 Mar 2000	Italy	6NC	Lansdowne Road	Won 60–13
479	19 Mar 2000	France	6NC	Stade de France	Won 27–25

480	1 April 2000	Wales	6NC	Lansdowne Road	Lost 19–23
481	3 June 2000	Argentina		Buenos Aires	Lost 23–34
482	10 June 2000	USA		Manchester	Won 83–3
483	17 June 2000	Canada		Markham	Drew 27–27
484	11 Nov 2000	Japan		Lansdowne Road	Won 78–9
485	19 Nov 2000	South Africa		Lansdowne Road	Lost 18–28
486	3 Feb 2001	Italy	6NC	Stadio Flaminio	Won 41–22
487	17 Feb 2001	France	6NC	Lansdowne Road	Won 22–15
488	2 June 2001	Romania		Bucharest	Won 37–3
489	22 Sept 2001	Scotland	6NC	Murrayfield	Lost 10–32
490	13 Oct 2001	Wales	6NC	Millennium Stadium	Won 36–6
491	20 Oct 2001	England	6NC	Lansdowne Road	Won 20–14
492	11 Nov 2001	Samoa		Lansdowne Road	Won 35–8
493	17 Nov 2001	New Zealand		Lansdowne Road	Lost 29–40
494	3 Feb 2002	Wales	6NC	Lansdowne Road	Won 54–10
495	16 Feb 2002	England	6NC	Twickenham	Lost 11–45
496	2 Mar 2002	Scotland	6NC	Lansdowne Road	Won 43–22
497	23 Mar 2003	Italy	6NC	Lansdowne Road	Won 32–17
498	6 April 2003	France	6NC	Stade de France	Lost 5–44
499	15 June 2002	New Zealand		Dunedin	Lost 6–15
500	22 June 2002	New Zealand		Eden Park	Lost 8–40
501	7 Sept 2002	Romania	WCQ	Thomond Park	Won 39–8
502	21 Sept 2002	Russia	WCQ	Krasnoyarsk	Won 35–3
503	28 Sept 2002	Georgia	WCQ	Lansdowne Road	Won 63–14
504	9 Nov 2002	Australia		Lansdowne Road	Won 18–9
505	17 Nov 2002	Fiji		Lansdowne Road	Won 64–17
506	23 Nov 2002	Argentina		Lansdowne Road	Won 16–7
507	16 Feb 2003	Scotland	6NC	Murrayfield	Won 36–6
508	22 Feb 2003	Italy	6NC	Stadio Flaminio	Won 37–13
509	8 Mar 2003	France	6NC	Lansdowne Road	Won 15–12
510	22 Mar 2003	Wales	6NC	Millennium Stadium	Won 25–24
511	30 Mar 2003	England	6NC	Lansdowne Road	Lost 6–42
512	7 June 2003	Australia		Perth	Lost 16–45
513	14 June 2003	Tonga		Nuku'alofa	Won 40–19
514	20 June 2003	Samoa		Apia	Won 40–14
515	16 Aug 2003	Wales		Lansdowne Road	Won 35–12

516	30 Aug 2003	Italy		Thomond Park	Won 61–6
517	6 Sept 2003	Scotland		Murrayfield	Won 29–10
518	11 Oct 2003	Romania	RWC	Gosford	Won 45–17
519	19 Oct 2003	Namibia	RWC	Sydney	Won 64–7
520	26 Oct 2003	Argentina	RWC	Adelaide	Won 16–15
521	1 Nov 2003	Australia	RWC	Melbourne	Lost 16–17
522	9 Nov 2003	France	RWC	Melbourne	Lost 21–43
523	14 Feb 2004	France	6NC	Stade de France	Lost 17–35
524	22 Feb 2004	Wales	6NC	Lansdowne Road	Won 36–15
525	6 Mar 2004	England	6NC	Twickenham	Won 19–13
526	20 Mar 2004	Italy	6NC	Lansdowne Road	Won 19–3
527	27 Mar 2004	Scotland	6NC	Lansdowne Road	Won 37–16
528	12 June 2004	South Africa		Bloemfontein	Lost 17–31
529	19 June 2004	South Africa		Cape Town	Lost 17–26
530	13 Nov 2004	South Africa		Lansdowne Road	Won 17–12
531	20 Nov 2004	USA		Lansdowne Road	Won 55–6
532	27 Nov 2004	Argentina		Lansdowne Road	Won 21–19
533	6 Feb 2005	Italy	6NC	Stadio Flaminio	Won 28–17
534	12 Feb 2005	Scotland	6NC	Murrayfield	Won 40–13
535	27 Feb 2005	England	6NC	Lansdowne Road	Won 19–13
536	12 Mar 2005	France	6NC	Lansdowne Road	Lost 19–26
537	19 Mar 2005	Wales	6NC	Millennium Stadium	Lost 20–32
538	12 June 2005	Japan		Osaka	Won 44–12
539	19 June 2005	Japan		Tokyo	Won 47–18
540	12 Nov 2005	New Zealand		Lansdowne Road	Lost 7–45
541	19 Nov 2005	Australia		Lansdowne Road	Lost 14–30
542	26 Nov 2005	Romania		Lansdowne Road	Won 34–12
543	4 Feb 2006	Italy	6NC	Lansdowne Road	Won 26–16
544	11 Feb 2006	France	6NC	Stade de France	Lost 31–43
545	26 Feb 2006	Wales	6NC	Lansdowne Road	Won 31–5
546	11 Mar 2006	Scotland	6NC	Lansdowne Road	Won 15–9
547	18 Mar 2006	England	6NC	Twickenham	Won 28–24
548	10 June 2006	New Zealand		Hamilton	Lost 23–34
549	17 June 2006	New Zealand		Eden Park	Lost 17–27

550	24 June 2006	Australia		Perth	Lost 15–37
551	11 Nov 2006	South Africa		Lansdowne Road	Won 32–15
552	19 Nov 2006	Australia		Lansdowne Road	Won 21–6
553	26 Nov 2006	Pacific Islands		Lansdowne Road	Won 61–17
554	4 Feb 2007	Wales	6NC	Millennium Stadium	Won 19–9
555	11 Feb 2007	France	6NC	Croke Park	Lost 17–20
556	24 Feb 2007	England	6NC	Croke Park	Won 43–13
557	10 Mar 2007	Scotland	6NC	Murrayfield	Won 19–18
558	17 Mar 2007	Italy	6NC	Stadio Flaminio	Won 51–24
559	26 May 2007	Argentina		Santa Fe	Lost 20–22
560	2 June 2007	Argentina		Buenos Aires	Lost 0–16
561	11 Aug 2007	Scotland		Murrayfield	Lost 21–31
562	24 Aug 2007	Italy		Ravenhill	Won 23–20